VAN(R
BOOK
Everything

Everything you wanted to know about
Vancouver and were going to ask anyway

Samantha Amara and
Beverly Cramp

MACINTYRE PURCELL PUBLISHING INC.

MacIntyre Purcell Publishing Inc.
232 Lincoln St., Suite D
PO Box 1142
Lunenburg, Nova Scotia
B0J 2C0
(902) 640-3350
www.bookofeverything.com
info@bookofeverything.com

Cover photo: istockphoto
123RF: page 88, 154
istockphoto: page 6, 20, 38, 66, 80, 104, 128, 174, 190

Printed and bound in Canada.

Library and Archives Canada Cataloguing in Publication
Amara, Samantha D. (Samantha Dawn), 1972-
Vancouver book of everything : everything you wanted to know about
Vancouver and were going to ask anyway / Samantha Amara, Beverly Cramp.
ISBN 978-0-9784784-7-6
1. Vancouver (B.C.). 2. Vancouver (B.C.)--Miscellanea. I. Cramp, Beverly II. Title.
FC3847.18.A53 2008   971.1'33
C2008-903310-8

Introduction

"Vancouver is lovely. There is no other word for it," wrote Sir Arthur Conan Doyle. And 100 plus years later he'd still be right. The most striking feature of Vancouver is her beauty. Like any great city, especially a frontier city on the edge of the continent, it has its mysteries. These are mysteries that can only be puzzled together by living here.

The philosophy behind the *Vancouver Book of Everything* is that a place is revealed by the accumulation of details. It is revealed one fact at a time, in the subtle nuances like the variations in weather and climate, pride and choice of its favourite sons and daughters, in the local slang, in the brutal crime or in the quiet park that only a tiny neighbourhood could harbour.

This is the city of Gassy Jack, Chris Haddock and Douglas Coupland. It is the city with the third largest Chinatown in North America and is the second most ethnic city on the continent. It is a city with frontier and blue-collar roots, but that now belongs firmly to the cosmopolitan mainstream. Vancouver is like great cities everywhere; it is a product of its contradictions. Our job and yours is to discover them.

We know no one book can really be about everything, of course. The toughest decisions are always not what to put in but rather what to leave out. And with each piece that didn't quite make the cut, we breathed a collective sigh of grief as it hit the floor, fingers crossed that it might make the next edition.

In a collaborative book such as this, there are a great many people to thank. Chuck Davis and Chris Mathieson offered intimate knowledge of the city. Beverly Cramp contributed her writing and personal insight. John MacIntyre for coming up with the Book of Everything concept. Thank you to Kelly Inglis for her editing and other assistance whenever needed, and especially to Martha Walls; her editorial direction was always thoughtful and patient. My husband Daniel, a special thank you for your support.

— Samantha Amara, August 2008

Table of Contents

Vancouver:

A Timeline

16,000 to 11,000 Before Present: The ancestors of British Columbia's Squamish, Tsleil-Waututh, Musqueam, Tsawwassen, Coquitlam, Katzie and Semiahmoo First Nations settle along Vancouver's coastlines, sustained by abundant wildlife and a hearty fishery.

1494: In the wake of news of Columbus' North American exploits of 1492, Spain signs the Treaty of Tordesillas, claiming the West Coast of North America from northern Mexico to Alaska.

1592-1774: A century after Columbus first spies North America, the Spanish travel the continent's West Coast, eventually settling at Nootka Sound on Vancouver Island. The Spanish legacy in the region lives on in place names such as the Strait of Juan de Fuca, the Spanish Banks and city streets such as Cordova, Cardero and Valdez.

1792: Britain's Captain George Vancouver sails into the Juan de Fuca Strait, becoming the first European to map the area. The same year Spain cedes her interest in the BC coast to Britain.

They Said It

1808: Explorer and fur trader Simon Fraser, thinking he is on the Columbia River, sails into Vancouver on the river that now bears his name.

1827: The Hudson's Bay Company (HBC) opens a trading post at Fort Langley on the Fraser River, marking the first permanent non-Native settlement in the area.

1858: Gold is discovered along the Fraser River, sparking the influx of thousands of prospectors.

1859: New Westminster, the region's first urban centre, is established.

1861: Greater Vancouver's first newspaper, the *British Columbian*, printed in New Westminster, is born.

1867: "Gassy Jack" Deighton opens a pub in his hotel on the Burrard Inlet. The establishment becomes popular with gold miners, fishers and forest workers and the area becomes known as Gastown.

1869: Gastown is incorporated as the new town of Granville.

1871: British Columbia joins Confederation.

1886: With a bustling population of about 1,000, the town of Granville is incorporated as the city of Vancouver in April. M.A. McLean is elected its first mayor.

1886: In May, a volunteer fire brigade is organized as one of the first orders of business in the newly incorporated city.

Bio CAPTAIN GEORGE VANCOUVER

When he first entered the British Royal Navy in 1771, George Vancouver could not have known he would be part of some of the greatest 18th century discovery expeditions. Within a year of joining the navy, Vancouver was appointed to Captain James Cook's ship the *Resolution* as Cook embarked on his second of three great discovery voyages.

From 1772 to 1775, Vancouver sailed with Cook to the south seas, and from 1776 to 1780 along the northwest coast in search of the fabled Northwest Passage. By the end of the 1780s, Vancouver had made his way up the chain of command and was part of a team preparing for an ambitious voyage to the south Pacific.

Just as this voyage was being planned, however, word reached London that the Spanish had commandeered British vessels at Nootka Sound (Vancouver Island) and set up shop. The incident nearly resulted in war, but Spain capitulated, signing over the area by treaty in 1790.

With the Nootka affair settled, Vancouver returned his attention to the surveying voyage to the south seas. En route, Vancouver was tasked with reclaiming for Britain property appropriated by Spain at Nootka and was instructed to survey the northwestern coast all the way to Alaska.

In completing this assignment, in June of 1792, Vancouver became the first European to sail into the Burrard Inlet. This feat was not forgotten. Ninety-four years later, when the town of Granville was incorporated in 1886, the newly minted West Coast city received a new name that was to taken to honour the sea captain who had first mapped the area for Britain.

1886: In June, fire set to burn brush gets out of control, swept by sudden wind gusts. Within an hour much of city, largely built of wood, is left a smoking ruin. The fire claims 880 buildings and 22 lives and compels city officials to mandate that all new buildings be built of flame-resistant brick or stone.

1887: A Canadian Pacific Railway (CPR) train makes its inaugural stop in Vancouver, the end of the line. The same year sees an anti-Chinese riot in city streets.

1888: Stanley Park officially opens.

Bio GASSY JACK

John "Gassy Jack" Deighton, a sailor, gold miner and saloon owner was the first European settler in the area that would grow to be Vancouver. Born thirty-seven years earlier in England, Deighton arrived on the shores of Burrard Inlet in 1867 and immediately began leaving his mark.

The one-time sailor followed the gold rush to the Fraser River in 1858. When this failed to pan out, Deighton opened the Globe saloon in New Westminster. Deighton's time at New Westminter was, however, cut short. In 1862 he chased another gold dream, entrusting his saloon to a friend while he was away. He returned to New Westminster to find his savings squandered. Bankrupt, Deighton decided to try his luck elsewhere.

It is said that within 24 hours of arriving in the wooded area that would be Vancouver, the entrepreneurial Deighton, with the help of men who worked in a nearby lumber mill, had built a new saloon, also named the Globe. The Globe stood at the site of what is now the corner of Water and Carrall streets.

The community that grew around the Globe became known as Gastown, after the enterprising first settler who, because of his pen-

They Said It

"[H]is name was a household word with most of our citizens."
— **From the obituary of Jack Deighton, the *Guardian*, 1875.**

1889: The first of three Granville Street bridges is built. The second replaces it in 1909 and the third in 1954.

1890: The city's first electric streetcars begin rolling.

1891: Vancouver's first public transit system takes fare-paying riders. Known as the Interurban, it consists primarily of trams.

chant for chatting (or "gassing") became known as Gassy Jack. Gastown was not for the faint of heart. First Nations people opposed the intrusion of settlers onto their land and animosities ran high. Deighton, however, got along quite well with the locals. He married twice, both times to Native women. With his second wife, Qua-Hail-Ya (Madeline) Deighton had a son, Richard.

As the community expanded, it became known officially as Granville, named after Earl Granville, Britain's colonial secretary. Although no longer its namesake, Deighton remained a formative citizen of the town. In 1870, he built Deighton House, a two-storey hotel and billiard parlor. He also took up the cause of ending lawlessness and joined other town leaders in a successful petition for a police officer.

Sadly, Jack Deighton did not see the further evolution of the town he had helped create. His health deteriorated and on May 29, 1875, forty-four-year-old Gassy Jack died. Six months later young Richard followed his father to the grave. Deighton House too succumbed, burning to the ground in the great fire of 1886. Deighton's wife, Qua-Hail-Ya, however, carried her husband's memory for many years. She lived to the age of 90 on the North Vancouver Indian Reserve.

1897-1898: The Klondike Gold Rush restores Vancouver's lagging economy, which had succumbed to a nation-wide recession in the mid-1890s.

Take 5 NANCY NOBLE'S TOP FIVE
OBJECTS AT THE VANCOUVER MUSEUM

Nancy Noble is the CEO of the Vancouver Museum, located in Vanier Park. The oldest and largest civic museum in the country (it has 100,000 artifacts), the Vancouver Museum holds a mirror up to the city and leads provocative conversations about its past, present and future.

1. **Mountain goat horn bracelet, Coast Salish, 18th century.** Thomas Dobson, a crewman aboard Captain George Vancouver's ship *HMS Discovery* collected this bracelet in 1792, an era of early encounter between the area's First Nations and Europeans. Descendants of the Coast Salish people who made this bracelet and traded it to Dobson still live in and around Vancouver. The bracelet is displayed in the Orientation Gallery.

2. **Maquette for the lion sculptures on the Lions Gate Bridge by sculptor Charles Marega, 1938.** Vancouver artist Charles Marega created stylized lions to guard each end of the Lions Gate Bridge. The bridge across the First Narrows of Burrard Inlet opened in 1939. Because it promised jobs in the height of the Great Depression, the bridge had the support of two-thirds of Vancouverites, even though it cut through Stanley Park. Two caissons weighing more than 2,000 tons each were sunk in the Narrows to support the southern end of the bridge and the deck hung from steel cables anchored in concrete blocks at each end. Originally Marega wanted to make the lions in bronze, but he settled for concrete. The scale model he created for the project is displayed in the Boom Bust War Gallery.

3. **Oldsmobile Runabout auto, 1906.** John Hendry, owner and operator of Hasting Sawmill, purchased this Oldsmobile "French Front" Runabout in 1906. Costing $750, it featured a wooden body and steel fender and was the 67th automobile registered in British Columbia.

1898: Rocky-shored English Bay in the city's downtown has sand shipped in to create its sandy beach.

Manufactured in a St. Catherine's, ON, factory, the Runabout featured the newest technology — a single cylinder internal combustion engine with a five-inch bore and six-inch stroke, developing seven horsepower. The planetary transmission had two forward speeds and one reverse. The car is displayed in the Gateway to the Pacific Gallery.

4. **Street photographer's camera, made and used by Foncie Pulice c.1935 to 1978.** Foncie Pulice of Foncie's Fotos was the best known of Vancouver's street photographers. He created a rolling sidewalk camera, modified to use camera-sized reels of film, so that he seldom had to pause to change film. Foncie photographed life on Granville and Hastings — the rich, the idle, the beautiful and the odd, friends, families, first dates, last dates, window shoppers and opera goers — Foncie's lens found them all. After snapping a candid shot, Foncie handed out a receipt. Photos could be picked up at his downtown studio the next day, in postcard or poster size. The camera is displayed in the 1950s Gallery.

5. **The Smilin' Buddha neon sign, designed and built by Wallace Neon c. 1950.** This is one of the most iconic pieces from Vancouver's colourful history of neon signs. When neon's popularity peaked in the late 1950s, the city glowed with over 19,000 signs. The Smilin' Buddha Cabaret on East Hastings Street, long a focal point of Vancouver's entertainment scene, was in the '50s a symbol of Vancouver's post-war prosperity and in the '60s psychedelic era hosted such acts as Jefferson Airplane and Jimi Hendrix. In the late 1970s, the Smilin' Buddha became home to Vancouver's punk and alternative music scene. In 1992, the Vancouver band 54-40 restored the sign and named their 1994 release *Smilin' Buddha Cabaret*. 54-40 donated the sign to the Vancouver Museum in 2007. It will be conserved and displayed in the So You Want a Revolution Gallery.

> "It is not difficult to imagine what the realization of such an undertaking would mean to the attractions of the park and personally I doubt if there exists anywhere on this continent such possibilities of a combined park and marine walk as we have in Stanley Park."
>
> **– Park Board Superintendent W. S. Rawling's**
> **vision for the seawall in 1918.**

1900: Vancouver's population surpasses that of the provincial capital of Victoria.

1907: Anti-Japanese sentiment culminates as non-Asian Vancouverites engage in the Vancouver Riot, leaving an enduring stain on the city for its intolerance of Japanese (and Asian) immigrants.

1907: The Vancouver Stock Exchange (VSE), a predecessor of Toronto's TSX Venture Exchange, begins operation. The VSE finances operations in the province for more than 90 years before merging with the Alberta Stock Exchange to create the Canadian Venture Exchange.

1908: The University of British Columbia is created by statute and in 1915 the institution holds its first classes.

1909: The city's first skyscraper, the Dominion Trust Building, rises above the city.

Did you know...

that when Terry Fox stopped his Marathon of Hope he had run 5,376 km and raised more than $24.17 million?

Man with a Dream

What has made Terry Fox one of the country's most enduring heroes was, strangely enough, his sheer ordinariness. Here was a humble, middle-class kid from Port Coquitlam who believed he could run across the second largest country in the world and somehow help raise money to find a cure for cancer.

In Douglas Coupland's wonderful book *Terry*, there is a photograph of the strikingly handsome Fox surrounded by a gaggle of young Newfoundland girls at a house party shortly after he dipped his foot in the Atlantic on April 12, 1980.

That was the way it began. Just Fox and his friend Doug Alward (who drove a van that they'd often sleep in unless they were offered a place to stay) and a dream. Alward would call ahead and try and get the local media to come out, sometimes with success, sometimes not.

Slowly, steadily, however, interest began to build. Folks began to show up on roadsides. Through Nova Scotia, New Brunswick and Quebec there were people starting to be curious. By the time Fox ran into Ottawa, it was for opening kick-off of a Rough Riders game and he was the star attraction.

Fox's journey now included a nation. Superstars like Bobby Orr and Darryl Sittler were asking for an audience with the young kid. (Sittler gave Fox his 1980 NHL All-Star team sweater.) As he rolled out of Toronto, 10,000 people lined the streets just to get a glimpse. Everywhere along Fox's route now, people were showing up shouting support, bringing their signs of "Go Terry Go."

On September 1, just outside Thunder Bay, a sharp pain that Fox had run through before returned, only this time it wouldn't go away. Bone cancer had spread to his lungs. He returned home to Vancouver. Canadians responded with a spontaneous outpouring of affection and commitment not seen before or since. Telethons and marathons, concerts and contests raised millions of dollars overnight.

When he died on June 28, 1981, the whole country mourned. What didn't die for any Canadian alive during that period was his spirit. People have always found ways to keep alive the memory of their heroes. They want their children to remember the clarity of that vision and purity of purpose that has the ability to move mountains. Canadians have made sure they've not forgotten and they honour that memory every year with the Terry Fox Run.

1911: The Arena, the first ice rink in Canada and then the largest in the world, opens. The same year, the city's first hockey team, the Vancouver Millionaires, lace up their skates.

1912: On February 12, the first edition of the *Vancouver Sun* rolls off the presses.

1915: The Vancouver Millionaires win Lord Stanley's Cup, defeating the Ottawa Senators.

1920: Harry Houdini hangs suspended from Vancouver's Sun Tower.

1925: The original Second Narrows Bridge joins Vancouver with North Vancouver.

1929: The municipalities of Point Grey and South Vancouver are annexed as part of the city of Vancouver.

1930: The Second Narrows Bridge goes out of operation for four years due to a major shipping accident. Prior to its reopening, the government purchases the bridge and installs a lift section.

1931: The Vancouver Art Gallery is established.

1936: Vancouver's current City Hall, located on Cambie and 12th Avenue, is dedicated.

1938: The Lions Gate Bridge opens to passengers, charging a toll of $0.25.

1942: Approximately 8,600 Japanese people living in Vancouver are removed from the BC coast by order of the federal government.

1948: Vancouver receives its first television broadcast from Seattle. Five years later the city gets its own TV station, CBUT.

1954: The 5th British Empire and Commonwealth Games are held in Vancouver.

1954: The BC Lions are created.

1957: Elvis Presley treats fans to a concert for the bargain price of two dollars. The King sings six songs and leaves the building after less than half an hour, leaving the crowd wanting more.

1958: Eighteen workers working on the Second Narrows Bridge are killed when several spans of the new bridge collapse, and a diver is killed days later while searching for bodies. The bridge is officially opened two years later.

1959: Vancouver's (and Canada's) first shopping mall, the Park Royal Shopping Centre, opens. The same year sees the opening of the Queen Elizabeth Theatre and the Maritime Museum, and the installation of the George Massey Tunnel that connects the towns of Richmond and Delta.

1963: Vancouver's port ranks first in tonnage shipped among all Canadian ports.

1964: The BC Lions win the Grey Cup.

1965: Simon Fraser University is established so quickly — the whole project takes a mere 18 months from start to finish — that it is dubbed "the instant university."

1970: The Vancouver Canucks play their inaugural game, losing to the Los Angeles Kings.

1976: The population of Greater Vancouver passes the one million mark.

1979: The Vancouver Whitecaps win the North American Soccer League championship.

1980: In September, after 60 years of on-again, off-again construction, the entire Stanley Park Seawall is completed and opens to the public.

1983: BC Place Stadium opens as the world's largest air-supported domed stadium. It seats 60,000 people and covers ten acres.

1985: To correct the growing traffic problems and the coming of the World Expo, Vancouver's SkyTrain, a two-line system on elevated tracks, makes its first run between Vancouver and New Westminster.

1986: Vancouver hosts the World Expo '86.

1988: Vancouver's first Gay Pride Festival is held.

1990: The city's first Indy car race revs through the downtown track. The event is held annually until 2004.

1994: On the evening of June 14, a riot erupts on downtown Vancouver streets after the Vancouver Canucks lose against the New York Rangers in Game 7 of the Stanley Cup finals. Damage is pegged at $1.1 million.

1994: The BC Lions win the Grey Cup.

1995: General Motors place opens, becoming a new home for the Vancouver Canucks and the newly incorporated Vancouver Grizzlies NBA team.

1995: The Ford Centre for the Performing Arts opens to the public; also the new Vancouver Public Library is built, reminiscent of a Roman Coliseum.

1997: On July 1, Hong Kong transfers to Chinese rule, ending 156 years of British control. The announcement of the changeover plan in 1984 prompts an estimated 100,000 Hong Kong Chinese to immigrate to Vancouver. To mark the changeover, pro-democracy demonstrators fly kites in city parks as a reminder of the precariousness of Hong Kong's freedom.

2002: The London-based *Economist* newsmagazine says Vancouver and Melbourne, Australia are the best cities in the world in which to live.

2003: On Canada Day, the International Olympic Committee announces that Vancouver will be the host city for the 2010 Olympic Winter Games and Paralympics.

2006: A December wind storm blows through Vancouver, ripping up more than 10,000 trees in Stanley Park — about 110 acres' worth — forcing the first complete closure of the park in more than 40 years.

2008: In May, a heist at UBC's Museum of Anthropology sees the theft of several very valuable pieces of work by Haida artist Bill Reid. All are later recovered, with only one piece having minor damage.

Vancouver Essentials

Origin of the Name: Named for British naval officer Captain George Vancouver. Searching for the Northwest Passage in 1792, Vancouver became one of the first Europeans to map North America's West Coast. Originally founded in the 1870s as the settlement of Granville, the new city was renamed after Vancouver upon its incorporation in 1886.

Coat of Arms: Granted in 1969, Vancouver's Coat of Arms honours the seaport with a shield containing a ship's sail and a crown, symbolic of the city's British connection. The top corners of the shield contain dogwood flowers, the provincial flower, while the Kwakiutl totem pole at the centre is a nod to the city's Aboriginal heritage. The city's motto spreads across the bottom.

Vancouver's Motto: "By sea, land and air we prosper."

Official Flag: The green chevron on the left side represents the land on which the city is built and the forest that has provided its prosperity. The alternating waving bars of blue and white symbolize the sea, Vancouver's other main source of wealth. The shield represents the city's status as a corporation. On the shield is the city badge, a specific mark of civic government.

Take 5 VANCOUVER'S TOP FIVE
ESSENTIAL TOURIST ATTRACTIONS

1. Stanley Park.
2. Granville Island.
3. Vancouver Aquarium.
4. Grouse Mountain.
5. Capilano Suspension Bridge.

Source: Tourism Vancouver.

Official Colours: Yellow, blue/purple and white

Official Flower: Rose

Official Band: Vancouver Police Pipe Band

Voting Age: 18

Drinking Age: 19

System of Measurement: Metric

Incorporated as a City: 1886

Time Zone: Pacific

Area Codes: 604 and 778

Postal Codes: V5K to V6Z

Did you know...

that according to Tourism Vancouver, 25,000 volunteers will help pull off the 2010 Olympic Games?

The People's Park

Vancouver's famous 1,000 acre park (named after Lord Stanley, the sitting Governor General and the same Lord Stanley for whom the Stanley Cup is named) is the third largest urban park in the country after Rouge Valley in Ontario (11,600 acres) and Wascana Park in Saskatchewan (2,325 acres), and is larger than New York's celebrated Central Park (843 acres) by more than 150 acres.

Stanley Park owes its existence to one of those all too rare flukes of history. Designated army reserve land, it was protected from development in case of an attack by the U.S. When that attack failed to materialize, the new city seized the opportunity to lease the land from the federal government. Stanley Park was officially opened on September 27, 1888, just two years after incorporation.

The park is the single most important landmark in the city. For the people of Vancouver it is that respite from the hustle and bustle of urban life, a connection to nature, an oasis and a place for contemplation. It is every bit as important to the psyche of the city as Central Park is to New York or Hyde Park to London. Stanley Park has been ranked as the sixteenth best park in the world and sixth best in North America by The Project for Public Spaces.

The park contains an estimated half million trees. Some are nearly 80 meters tall, others nearly three centuries old. There are over 200 km of walkways, roads and hiking trails. The park is also home to modern contrivances such as restaurants, theatres, the Vancouver Aquarium and the city's largest water park.

One of its most notable features is the 8.8 km seawall, built over six decades to prevent seaside erosion. In the 1970s when the last pieces of the wall were constructed, the city paved its top and in 1980 it was open to walkers, bikers and rollerbladers.

When a massive windstorm felled more than 10,000 trees in the park in December of 2006, it was like a death in family. For the first time in more than 40 years the park was closed to the public. In less than a year, however, more than 7,000 private citizens and corporations stepped up with financial support and that, along with support from all levels of government, launched a massive $9.5 million restoration project. In short order the park roads and trails were reopened and the seawall repaired.

They Said It

Statutory Holidays: Vancouver's statutory holidays are in keeping with those across Canada. They are New Year's Day, Good Friday, Easter Monday, Victoria Day, Canada Day, Civic Holiday (the first Monday of August), Labour Day, Thanksgiving Day, Remembrance Day, Christmas Day and Boxing Day.

Sister Cities: Los Angeles, Guangzhou, Yokohama, Edinburgh, Odessa

Metro Vancouver: Unlike many Canadian cities, Vancouver has resisted amalgamation. This means that Greater Vancouver has 22 member municipalities, one of which is Vancouver proper.

POPULATION

Vancouver is British Columbia's largest city. In 2006, the population of Vancouver proper reached 578,041 and that of the Census Metropolitan Area (the CMA, which includes outlying municipalities) of Vancouver hit 2,116,581, making the West Coast city Canada's third largest after Toronto and Montreal. Vancouver CMA is home to about half of all British Columbians, and has almost as many people as the countries of Bhutan (2.2 million) and Latvia (2.2 million). If Vancouver was an American city it would fall somewhere between Houston (2.0 million) and Chicago (2.8 million). Twice as many people live in Vancouver as in Nova Scotia and there are more than 72 times more people in the Vancouver CMA than there are in the entire territory of Nunavut.

Take 5 VANCOUVER PUBLIC LIBRARY'S
FIVE ESSENTIAL VANCOUVER READS

This list was generated from a number of Vancouver Public Library staff members. They were quick to point out that the list is by no means definitive and that they have many other suggestions.

1. *Dream City: Vancouver and the Global Imagination* (2005), Lance Berelowitz. The story behind Vancouver's emerging urban form: the buildings, public spaces, extraordinary landscapes and cultural values that have turned the city into the poster-child of North American urbanism.

2. *City of Glass: Douglas Coupland's Vancouver* (2000), Douglas Coupland. The book looks at Vancouver from inside out, from the Grouse Grind to the shimmering glass towers, First Nations to feng-shui. Douglas Coupland takes on monster houses, weather, Sandra Bernhard, Love Boats, SkyTrain, fleece, that endless rivalry with Seattle, and even includes a short story about living in a low-rent Granville hotel.

3. *The Jade Peony* (1995), Wayson Choy. This wonderful book is about growing up in Vancouver's early Chinatown in the 1930s and '40s, narrated in three sections by three children from the same family.

4. *Vancouver: An Illustrated History* (1980), Patricia E. Roy. This book shows how in the course of a single century Vancouver rose from being a clearing in the forest to one of the most beautiful and cosmopolitan cities on the continent.

5. *Vancouver: A Visual History* (1992), Bruce MacDonald. Fourteen historical maps from each decade from the 1850s to the 1980s allow you to compare the physical and demographic changes in the city. Notes and a historical summary accompany each map, followed by a double page of highlights from each decade, including capsule biographies of remarkable people—some of them famous, others relatively unknown.

YOU KNOW YOU'RE FROM

- You have a sun lamp in your rec room to help you through those sun-less winter days.
- You have never spent money on curl enhancers for your hair.
- Your parka gets worn exactly once a year — on your annual trek to the mountains.
- The peaches you had for breakfast are super fresh; you picked them from the tree on your front lawn.
- Your 3-bedroom, single bath bungalow is worth as much as a mansion just about anywhere else in Canada.
- You drank green tea long before it became trendy.
- Your friend of a friend of a friend went to school with Bryan Adams.
- You like your vendor hotdog served with seaweed.
- Your commute involves a ferry ride.
- You wrote your first novel in three days at a Three-Day Novel-Writing Contest, a phenomenon that you know was born in your hometown.
- You know what it means to take a walk on The Drive.
- You know that there is no such thing as "South Van."
- You are no longer phased by movie-star sightings.
- You consider Winnipeg to be "out east."
- You go to English Bay to watch fireworks.
- You had your morning cuppa at Blenz and your afternoon hit of caffeine at J.J. Bean House.
- You can be at one Robson Street Starbucks and wave to a friend at another Starbucks across the street.
- You own a pair of Spank shoes.
- You have been called a Canuckle head.
- Farmed salmon just doesn't cut it.
- You have no winter driving skills. None.

VANCOUVER WHEN . . .

- In the winter you can play a round of golf in the morning and go skiing in the afternoon.
- You are annoyed rather than curious when navigating around a movie shoot underway on a downtown street.
- You've always heard that the city is too young to have heritage — and then you read about a 100-year-old house being demolished.
- Your daily jog through Stanley Park takes you past palm trees.
- Your former office building downtown has been converted to condos.
- Your local Canadian Tire just sells all-seasons.
- You plan to make a killing by renting out your house in the winter of 2010.
- Your summer of 2007 stunk. Literally.
- People from away are surprised to learn that you do not, in fact, wear socks and sandals.
- You know that the west side, the West End, and West Vancouver are not the same area.
- Your lunch spot of choice is White Spot.
- You can't figure out what the big deal is about the Steam Clock.
- Pals in Toronto are surprised to learn that neither you, nor your friends, smoke marijuana.
- You can spot cruise ship visitors from a mile away.
- You often catch a few ZZZZZs on the SkyTrain.
- You find yourself rooting for Quila's baby.
- Your favourite Subway sandwich includes the vegetarian patty.
- You've been warned ad nauseum about the "Big One" that is coming and you are oddly unconcerned.
- Your January wardrobe includes shorts.
- You have a plethora of umbrellas scattered about at work, at home and in the car, "just in case."

POPULATION GROWTH

Between 2001 and 2006 the population of the Vancouver CMA grew by 6.5 percent. The fastest growing municipality within the CMA was Surrey, followed by Vancouver, Richmond and Burnaby. Greater Vancouver is expected to reach a population of 2.6 million by 2021 and hit the 3 million mark by 2031.

Sources: Canada Legal Information Services; Statistics Canada; Greater Vancouver Regional Development.

 JEN SOOKFONG LEE'S FIVE
BEST THINGS ABOUT LIVING IN VANCOUVER

Born and raised in East Vancouver, Jen Sookfong Lee's well-received first novel, *The End of East* (Knopf Canada, New Face of Fiction 2007) spans almost the entire 20th century as it delves into the underside of Chinese Canadian history through the eyes of the Chan family. Lee is also involved in Vancouver's literary scene and has co-hosted CBC's Studio One Book Club.

1. **Weather.** There are few places in Canada where you're not waist-deep in snow in January or eaten alive by mosquitoes in July. While Vancouver has a reputation for rain, rain and more rain, the benefit of this temperate rainforest is that it is never too cold that you can't hike outside or too hot that you can't sun yourself on the back deck.

2. **The food.** Vancouver has a mind-boggling number of restaurants per capita, rumoured to be the highest in the country. Vancouver is famous for Asian food, especially Chinese and Japanese which is widely touted as the best outside of Asia. Included in our culinary arsenal are some of the highest profile restaurants in Canada: Lumière, West, Bishop's, Vij's and Tojo's.

3. **The diversity.** The face of the city is constantly changing and this has an enormous effect on how well Vancouverites live with one

POPULATION BY AGE AND SEX

AGE	MALES	FEMALES	TOTAL	PERCENTAGE
0-14	178,190	167,545	345,735	16
15-24	144,760	140,945	285,705	14
25-44	308,405	329,080	637,485	30
45-64	282,240	294,375	576,615	27
65+	119,285	152,150	271,435	13

Source: Statistics Canada.

another and how far we're willing to go to understand our neighbours. Families here are often multi-ethnic, proving that people of different backgrounds can always find common ground.

4. **The landscape.** Vancouver wouldn't be Vancouver without the ocean, mountains and trees. In downtown's Stanley Park, it's easy to disappear into the woods for a whole day and forget you're in the middle of a large, bustling city. The north shore mountains are a short drive away for skiers and snowboarders, and for those who like their recreation a little saltier, Burrard Inlet, English Bay and the Strait of Georgia surround the city on three sides.

5. **The history.** Vancouver has always been a primary industry town. Men working in the logging, mining and fishing industries came to town to spend their off-hours in what was once known as Gastown. As a result Vancouver was, at the end of the 19th, and in during much of the 20th century, a kind of sin city. Add to this mix the large immigrant communities who were not always welcomed, and you have a colourful, sometimes shameful, history. Vancouver had it all: burlesque, opium, larger than life madams and gangsters, race riots, and a police force only occasionally motivated to crack down on it all.

POPULATION IN PERSPECTIVE (2006)

- Calgary (CMA)   1,079,310
- Ottawa-Gatineau (CMA)   1,130,761
- **Vancouver (CMA)**   **2,116,581**
- Montreal (CMA)   3,635,571
- Toronto (CMA)   5,113,149
- New York City   21,976,224

Source: Statistics Canada.

POPULATION DENSITY (PEOPLE/KM²)

- New York City   10,194
- Toronto   3,939
- **Vancouver**   **735.6**
- British Columbia   4.4
- Canada   3.5

Source: Greater Vancouver Regional Development.

FERTILITY RATE (PER WOMAN, 2006)

Vancouver:	**1.0**
British Columbia:	1.4
Canada:	1.5

Source: Statistics Canada.

Did you know...

that Vancouver currently has the second largest trolley bus fleet in North America after San Francisco?

Did you know...

that according to Heifer International, an organization aimed at ending world hunger, 44 percent of Vancouverites grow fruits, vegetables, berries, nuts or herbs in their yards or on their balconies?

Take CHUCK DAVIS' TOP FIVE
HIGHLIGHTS IN VANCOUVER HISTORY

Historian Chuck Davis has been writing on Vancouver's history for more than 30 years. With hundreds of newspaper columns and 15 books to his name, Davis is currently working on what he calls the capstone of his writing career, *The History of Metropolitan Vancouver.*

1. **The Great Fire.** On June 13, 1886, just weeks after its incorporation, Vancouver burned to the ground when a fire set to burn slash roared out of control, leaving an estimated 22 dead. City pioneers began to rebuild while the embers were still warm.

2. **The arrival of the railway.** The choice of Vancouver as the terminus for the Canadian Pacific Railway ensured the town's dominant role in southwestern BC. Appropriately, the first passenger to step from the first train onto the platform on May 23, 1887, was a young Welshman named Jonathan Rogers, who, in later years, became a prominent Vancouver developer and philanthropist. The CPR received a huge swath of town as a reward for extending its line from Port Moody.

3. **The creation of Stanley Park.** The first decision of Vancouver's first city council was to request from the federal government the lease of a 1,000-acre military reserve to be used as a park. A little over two years later Mayor David Oppenheimer presided over the opening of Stanley Park, one of the largest civic parks in the world and Vancouver's most important landmark.

4. **The Strathcona Protest.** In October of 1967, the residents of the predominantly Chinese Strathcona neighborhood in the East End were outraged by city plans to level 600 homes and bypass Chinatown by running a freeway through their neighborhood. Their protests succeeded and the plans were dropped.

5. **Expo '86.** The decision to hold a world exposition in Vancouver in 1986 to coincide with the city's centennial was controversial. (Vancouver Mayor Mike Harcourt was a notable opponent). The six-month exposition (opened in May by Prince Charles and Princess Diana) was expected to attract 14 million, but ended up drawing 22 million and earning Vancouver an international profile. It was a heck of a show.

"Vancouver is lovely. There is no other word for it."
– Sir Arthur Conan Doyle, author and traveler
in *Our Second Adventure* (1923).

LIFE EXPECTANCY
Vancouverites live longer than Canadians living in any other CMA.

Canada	79.4
Vancouver	**81.1**
Toronto	81.0
Edmonton	79.8
Montreal	79.5
Halifax	79.1
Regina	78.0
Sudbury	76.7

Source: Statistics Canada.

HEALHTY CITY

	Vancouver	Canada
Percentage who smoke	15.5	24
Percentage who drink heavily	12.0	15
Percentage who are physically inactive	37.7	50
Percentage who have high blood pressure	10.7	12
Percentage who are obese	10.7	15

Source: Canadian Community Health Survey.

Did you know...

that at 137 m long and 70 m high, the Capilano Bridge is the longest and highest suspended footbridge in the world?

Take 5   KAREN QUINN FUNG'S FIVE

ESSENTIAL FREE (OR CHEAP) THINGS
TO DO IN VANCOUVER

We all know that students on budgets learn to find freebies, and Karen Quinn Fung is no exception. In her six years as a communication student at Simon Fraser University, Quinn has some of the most highly developed penny-pinching skills in the city. Here are some of her tips for seeing Vancouver for free, or darn close to it.

1. **Summer Night Markets.** Held on Friday and Saturday nights, these markets are summertime staples in Vancouver's Chinatown and in Richmond. Buy products from around the world and bring your appetite for food stands flowing with unique desserts and low-priced finger foods. Save even more money — take the bus and avoid traffic congestion.

2. **Public Dreams Society.** If it's the last week of July or Halloween, make or borrow a costume and head to Trout Lake for Illuminaries Festival of Lanterns or The Parade of Lost Souls: two all-night creative public celebrations.

3. **The UBC Museum of Anthropology.** The MOA specializes in the histories of British Columbia's First Nations. Come on a Tuesday between 5 pm and 9 pm when admission is just a flat fiver. The trek is also a great excuse to check out the UBC campus, particularly the work of architect Arthur Erickson.

4. **The Bloedel Conservatory.** The Bloedel Conservatory, located in Queen Elizabeth Park, is the climate controlled home to over 100 species of birds and tropical plants, all for the bargain basement entrance fee of $4.60 for an adult. The park boasts a panoramic view of the city and also features a duck pond and cherry trees that are dripping in blossoms in the spring.

5. **Critical Mass.** Vancouver has a thriving cycling community. For free, you can join hundreds of cyclists in a mass bike ride. Bike sculptures, costumes and the views as you cross local bridges make this experience one of a kind. Cyclists (and rollerbladers) assemble for these rides on the lawn of the Vancouver Art Gallery on the last Friday of each month.

Take 5 TOP FIVE ETHNIC ORIGINS
CLAIMED BY VANCOUVERITES (2006)

1. **British Isles:** 753,215
2. **East and South East Asian:** 584,895
3. **Western European:** 289,030
4. **South Asian:** 208,535
5. **Southern European:** 172,420

Source: Statistics Canada.

MEDIAN AGE

BC	40.2 years
Vancouver	**39.1 years**
Men	38.3 years
Women	39.3 years

GOLDEN YEARS

In all, 13 percent of Vancouverites are 65 or older. The oldest community in the CMA is White Rock, where 28 percent of the population is over 65 and the youngest is Anmore, where just six percent of the people are in their golden years.

GIRLS AND BOYS

- Percentage of Vancouverites who are male: 48.8
- Female: 51.2

Source: Statistics Canada.

FIRST COMES MARRIAGE

- Marriage rate (per 1,000 population) in BC   5.3
- Marriage rate in Prince Edward Island, the highest 6.0
- Marriage rate in Quebec, the lowest   2.8
- Canada's marriage rate   4.7

Source: Statistics Canada.

D-I-V-O-R-C-E

- Rate of divorce (per 100 marriages) in BC   44.7
- Divorce rate in Quebec, the highest   49.7
- Divorce rate in Prince Edward Island, the lowest 27.3
- Canada's divorce rate   38.3

Source: Statistics Canada.

NEWCOMERS

Forty percent of all Vancouverites are immigrants — up from 29 percent in 1986. The community in the Greater Vancouver area with the highest immigrant population is Richmond at 57 percent, followed by Burnaby (51 percent), Vancouver (46 percent) and Surrey (38 percent).

By comparison, nearly 46 percent of people living in the Toronto CMA, 24 percent of people in the Calgary CMA and 21 percent living in the Montreal CMA are immigrants, with 19 percent, 23 percent and 22 percent, respectively, having arrived between 2001 and 2006.

Sources: BC Statistics; Statistics Canada.

RELIGIOUS AFFILIATION

Roman Catholic	18.5 percent
United Church	8.6 percent
Anglican	6.8 percent
Sikh	4.5 percent
Buddhist	4.0 percent
Baptist	2.5 percent
Muslim	2.5 percent
Hindu	1.3 percent
Jewish	0.9 percent

Did you know...

that on April 24, 1872, Gassy Jack Deighton flew the first Canadian flag ever on the Burrard Inlet when he raised it above Deighton House?

Pentecostal	0.86 percent
Greek Orthodox	0.57 percent
Jehovah's Witnesses	0.56 percent
Mormon	0.26 percent
Pagan	0.15 percent

Source: Statistics Canada.

VANCOUVER IS HOME TO

- The second largest K-12 school system in BC with 56,000 fulltime students, 91 elementary schools, 18 secondary schools and seven adult education centres
- 20 private and public colleges
- Two research universities
- 58 vocational/career-oriented institutions
- 30 private language schools operate in Vancouver, most of them focusing on English as a second language instruction

HIGHER LEARNING

Vancouver is internationally renowned for excellence in education and each year attracts nearly 150,000 international students to its post-secondary institutions, lured by the high quality of education and by recent regulations that have made it easier for international students to work in BC upon graduation.

Vancouver's University of British Columbia is consistently ranked in the world's top 50. In 2007, the *Times Higher Education* rankings placed UBC 33rd and *Maclean's* annual university ranking named Simon Fraser University top among mid-sized institutions in Canada for medical and science grants, faculty awards, and social science and humanities grants and second for overall academic excellence.

Did you know...

that according to Statistics Canada, 52 percent of city residents and 43 percent of Metro residents have a first language other than English?

HEALTH CARE

- Hospitals/Acute Care: 13
- Diagnostic Treatment Centres: 3
- Number of beds: 8,936
- Number of doctors: 3,128

Sources: Vancouver Coastal Health; College of Physicians and Surgeons of BC; Canadian Medical Association.

PROFESSIONAL SPORTS

Vancouver is home to four professional sports franchises. The Vancouver Canucks hockey team plays out of General Motors Place, the BC Lions play out of BC Place Stadium, the Vancouver Canadians baseball club's home turf is Nat Bailey Stadium and the Vancouver Whitecaps FC soccer club use the pitch at Swangard Stadium.

Weblinks

City of Vancouver Website

vancouver.ca

Find out city government, services and much more at this site maintained by the City of Vancouver.

Volunteer Vancouver

www.volunteervancouver.ca

Find out how to get involved in city life.

Vancouver Cams

www.vancouver.com/community/webcams/

Check out any number of community web cams, in real time.

Did you know...

that in 2006, Vancouver was voted the world's most attractive destination based on livability according to *The Economist* Economist Intelligence Unit (EIU)? Vancouver beat out Melbourne (second) and Vienna (third).

Slang:

Vancouverites, like people the world over, have a 'lingo' unique to their place. These words have been nurtured and given meaning over time. They inform our jokes, reflect our histories and cultures and give our conversations familiar shorthand. Vancouver is blessed by a rich dialect — some is shared by neighbouring West Coast communities, but much is distinct. Here is a small sample.

BC Bud: BC Bud is high quality marijuana and is often referred to as the province's most important cash crop.

Bugs on the Bridge: Refers to outrageous stunts performed annually by engineering students at the University of British Columbia. In 1982, 1994 and in 2008, precocious students demonstrated their engineering acumen by suspending Volkswagen Beetle cars from the Lion's Gate Bridge.

Canuckle Head: The derisive nickname for a fan of the Vancouver Canucks NHL team.

Cultch, The: Once a church, this is the nickname for the Vancouver East Cultural Centre, a cultural treasure and one of the city's most unique performance spaces.

Dayliner: Diesel-powered passenger railcar once common on the British Columbia Railway.

Doeskin: A thick black and red flannel lumber jacket originally worn by lumberers or miners.

F.O.B.: Old acronym for the derogatory phrase 'fresh off the boat;' historically used to denote a new immigrant.

Fantasy Garden World: This defunct Richmond theme park featuring heavy doses of Christian fundamentalism was the brain child of former Premier Bill Vander Zalm. The park had much to do with Vander Zalm's political undoing as there were conflict-of-interest concerns about his plans to sell it. The park was sold in 2007 and is slated for demolition.

Front, The: A nickname for the Western Front, an artist-run centre established in 1973 as an artists' collective. Known for its experimental art, the Front produces over 100 shows annually.

Garage, The: Nickname for GM Place, the arena home of the Vancouver Canucks that refers to the arena's sponsor, General Motors.

Gracie's Necklace: When the Lions Gate Bridge was illuminated in 1986 to celebrate Expo, it was at the behest of provincial MLA, Grace McCarthy. The bridge's graceful looping cables light up like a string of pearls at night, said early reports.

Grouse Grind: A popular and grueling 2.9 km hike up Grouse Mountain. The trek is rewarded with amazing views of the city and English Bay.

Hollywood North: A reference to Vancouver as it emerged as a centre of North American film and TV production in 1980s. Only LA and New York make more films.

Take 5 POET LAUREATE GEORGE MCWHIRTER'S FIVE BEST
WORDS TO DESCRIBE VANCOUVER)

George McWhirter is currently Vancouver's Inaugural Poet Laureate. He has lived there with his wife, Angela, since 1968. His latest book, *The Incorrection* (Oolichan Books) begins on Jericho Beach and Spanish Banks. His next, *The Anachronicles* (Ronsdale Press) ends there, at Wreck Beach.

1. **Snow**
2. **rain-mountain**
3. **sea-drugged**
4./5. **Phantasmagarden**

Why these five? Vancouver is hard used by two drugs: its beauty and the heroin that pours through the Port of Vancouver. Pollen is blown, even thicker than the heroin on Vancouver streets because Vancouverites are addicted to gardens, and the increase in exotic botanical species has turned it into the floral and arboreal ghost or simulacrum of almost everywhere else in the world. Every morning the eyes note the snow line on the mountains, which are seen even better from the East End, or they check the level of rain in the gauge nailed to the back porch. The indigenous music of Vancouver is rain. Like interest in a bio-botanical bank, everything gets compounded and grows in Vancouver. Everyone in the city is fully invested in it. Hence the three compound words, two hyphenated.

Interior, The: That part of British Columbia that is outside of Greater Vancouver, the Islands and the North Coast. Also refers to the divide between largely urban and rural communities (the interior representing the rural).

Island, The: Vancouver Island.

Take 5 INNKEEPER EVAN PENNER'S TOP FIVE "OFF THE BEATEN TRACK" THINGS TO DO IN VANCOUVER

The house that is home to the West End Guest House on Haro Street was built with pure straight-grained cedar in 1906. The building has gone through many owners and décors since, but has always maintained a dignity and presence in the heart of the city's posh West End. Evan Penner has been the establishment's innkeeper since 1991.

1. Gondola up Grouse Mountain and tandem parasailing down. To get a real sense of the city, first time visitors to Vancouver should go to our best vantage point: Grouse Mountain. If you have a few extra bucks, try parasailing down over the homes perched on the side of the mountain and then land in the field below.

2. Rent a small boat and sail up Indian Arm and see the quieter side of Vancouver. Vancouver is best seen by water so sail Burrard Inlet, past freighters, the Seabus, a cruise ship, sea planes and the Second Narrows Bridge. At this point, the scenery gets more serene. If you go left at the first island past Caits Park in North Vancouver, you will find yourself in Deep Cove where you can take in some of the amazing homes lining the Cove — most of which are accessible only by water. Farther on, you will see the now defunct Buntzen Power Plant. At the end of the inlet is the Wigwam Inn. A German Biergarten in the heydays before WWI, it was in the 1970s a place the paddle wheeler from Coal Harbour stopped for "Tea." It is now owned by the Royal Vancouver Yacht Club (they don't like you to dock, but you can have a look from the boat).

Islands, The: The collective name for British Columbia's Gulf Islands.

Japa Dog: A street corner vendor hotdog, Vancouver style. Rather than mustard and ketchup, this wildly popular tasty treat is served Japanese style, with such toppings as teriyaki sauce, Japanese mayo and nori, a seaweed.

3. Sea plane ride around the harbour. This is another great way to see Vancouver. Fly over Stanley Park, check out multi-million dollar homes in West Vancouver, see Horseshoe Bay where the ferries dock and then head back towards UBC campus. Keep an eye out for the various beaches of Kitsilano, Jericho and Spanish Banks before heading back over the downtown office buildings. With this bird's eye view, you can see why the West End, Coal Harbour and Yaletown are so densely populated. When you land on the water near the new convention centre — be sure to check out its strawberry roof.

4. A quiet walk through Southlands where you can find horse paddocks and take a little jump back into 19th century upper middle class English lifestyle. Vancouver is very vibrant, but there still is room for the gentile life in Southlands. On the shores of the Fraser River, near its mouth, across from the airport, you'll find impressive homes, with stables and corrals, country lanes with ditches instead of side walks and some access to the river's dyke. This is prime territory on which to stop and enjoy a picnic.

5. A trip to historic Fort Langley. This is a great way to experience local history and appreciate the importance of the Hudson's Bay Company to the province's evolution. Located on the banks of the Fraser River and with the mountains in the background, it is quite picturesque. The little village nearby is a good spot to enjoy a piece of homemade dessert, fish and chips, or a drink in a local pub.

L.D.B: The Liquor Distribution Board, purveyors of all things booze on the West Coast.

Left Coast: The Canadian West Coast of which Vancouver is part, so-named because of the large proportion of people adhering to the left side of political spectrum.

Lotus-Land: A nickname for Vancouver reflecting the idea that its citizens are laid-back and enjoy an uncharacteristically temperate Canadian climate and beautiful surroundings. It can also refer to the perception that Vancouverites engage in wide numbers in a new age culture based on Eastern philosophies and practices.

Nucks: Term of endearment for the Vancouver Canucks.

Over town: What people in the North Shore municipalities of Vancouver call Vancouver Proper.

Pac Press: Pacific Press, who used to own both Vancouver's major daily newspapers (the *Vancouver Sun* and *The Province*). Although it is now owned by a media conglomerate and the name has changed, locals still refer to the papers and the company as Pac Press.

Pain and Wastings: The sad nickname for the intersection of Main and Hastings, the centre of the notorious Lower Eastside.

Queen E, The: The Queen Elizabeth Theatre. Home to the Vancouver Opera, it is one of Vancouver's premiere performance venues.

Salt Chuck: The Pacific Ocean. A term taken from an old Chinook pidgin trade language, Chuck is water and salt chuck, the ocean.

FIVE WAYS VANCOUVERITES
DESCRIBE RAIN

1. **Mist:** very light rain with precipitation rates less than .25 mm/hr
2. **Showers:** light rain when precipitation rates are roughly between .25 – 1 mm/hour
3. **Flurries:** bouts of rain with precipitation rates roughly between 1 – 2 mm/hour
4. **Downpours:** periods of rain with precipitation rates roughly between 2 – 10 mm/hour
5. **Rainstorms:** rain with precipitation rates over 10 mm/hour

Skookum: A well-used Chinook term meaning strong, swift, first-rate, well-made or awesome.

SkyTrain: Not quite as high flying as it sounds, the SkyTrain is Vancouver's automated rapid transit system. Built for the 1986 World Fair, SkyTrain continues to expand as the 2010 Olympics loom. With nearly 50 km of track, it is the longest rapid transit system on the planet.

Slurrey: Derogatory term for Surrey that reflects outsiders' conceptions of Surrey as a "hard" town.

Squamish Winds/Squamishes: High winds that blow out of a West Coast channel or valley, especially in winter.

Squatch: Derived from the word Sasquatch, it refers to a tall and unkempt individual with a shaggy beard.

Straight, The: Founded as an anti-establishment alternative newspaper in 1967, *The Georgia Straight* has is now popular Vancouver weekly arts and entertainment newspaper known simply as *The Straight*.

Surrey Girl: An insult aimed at a young woman who is loud-mouthed and unsophisticated. These traits are derogatorily said to be the product of life in Surrey, a Greater Vancouver community stereotyped as being rough and tumble.

Tube, The: The George Massey Tunnel.

Terminal City: Another nickname for Vancouver that reflects its place at the end, or the terminus, of the Canadian railway system.

TUTS: The handle given to the Theatre Under the Stars, which began back in 1934. It features the outdoor band shell in Stanley Park which became a performance place for one of Vancouver's largest musical theatre companies which produces two musicals during the summer.

Vag, the: Rhyming with bag, this is the nickname for the Vancouver Art Gallery, the largest gallery in Western Canada.

Van: Local short form used for Vancouver as well as its districts e.g. East Van, West Van and North Van. Note: there is no South Van.

Vancouverite: One from Vancouver.

Vancouver Special: A boxy house style, with the main living area above the first floor that flourished in the 1970s. Vancouver Specials are characterized by the absence of a basement and with a balcony railing across the front of the second floor of the home (but no balcony).

Wet Coast: A play on the term West Coast that reflects the copious rainfall Vancouver enjoys each year.

White Spot: A popular West Coast restaurant chain that was founded in Vancouver in 1928 by Nat Bailey.

Zalm Thought: A malapropism; the type that the exuberant and eccentric former Premier Bill Vander Zalm (1986-1991) was known for. (See: Fantasy Garden World)

Weblinks

CBC's 5000 New Words
www.cbc.ca/news/background/language/
Some of the newest words to make it into Canadian English.

George McWhirter
www.city.vancouver.bc.ca/commsvcs/oca/Awards/poet/current.htm
Find out more about Vancouver's first Poet Laureate!

Urban Geography

IN THE BEGINNING

Beginning approximately 200 to 300 million years ago, a group of islands in the Pacific ocean began to move northeast on the back of the Pacific plate, where they collided with the North American plate and fused into the region we now know as mainland British Columbia. About 150 million years ago, molten rock strained deep beneath the earth's crust and 70 million years later, this pressure caused the earth-quakes and volcanic eruptions that gave birth to the Coast Mountains. Beginning in the Fraser Valley and stretching north to Alaska, these mountains provide the backdrop to modern day Vancouver.

While this earth-shattering action gave rise to the mountains, the Cordilleran ice sheet that covered most of the southern portion of the province until about 15,000 years ago, gave them their character, scraping and shaping the land. As it inched away from the site of present day Vancouver and as ice melted into the Fraser River, this glacier (up to 2 km thick in places) left behind the clay, mud and rocks that is the physical foundation of the city and carved the picturesque u-shaped valleys characteristic of the Vancouver area today.

AREA (KM^2)

	CMA	City Proper
Toronto	5,903	630
Montreal	4,047	186
Vancouver	**2,879**	**115**
Halifax	5,490	97

WATER BOUND

Surrounded by water, Vancouver is framed to the north by the Burrard Inlet, which serves as its main harbour and separates it from the communities of North and West Vancouver, as well as the Coast Mountains. The Fraser River marks the south border of the city, separating it from the communities of Richmond and Delta, while on its western shores lie English Bay and the Pacific Ocean.

ELEVATION

Most of Metro Vancouver is within one metre of sea level, with parts of it, Richmond, for example, being below sea level. Vancouver's terrain varies widely, however, with Grouse Mountain rising more than 1,100 m above the city.

LONGITUDE AND LATITUDE

Vancouver is located at 49 16' N latitude and 123 07' W longitude. These coordinates put the city along the same latitude as Budapest, Munich, Paris and Zurich, and along the longitude similar to such places as Seattle, San Francisco and Tijuana.

Did you know...

that more than 8 million people visit Stanley Park each year?

HERE AND THERE

Vancouver is:

- 4,412 km from Toronto
- 5,970 km from Halifax
- 4,721 km from Montreal
- 977 km from Calgary
- 2,152 km from Winnipeg
- 105 km from Victoria
- 50 km from the United States border

A River Runs Near It

The Fraser River, the longest in British Columbia and the tenth longest in Canada, stretches 1,400 km from the Rockies to empty into the Pacific near Vancouver. Little did explorer Simon Fraser know when he first followed it that this ancient waterway would, within a century, become home to one of the world's most successful metropolises.

On its route from the Rockies, into BC's interior, on to the Coast Mountains and then to the Fraser River Valley and Pacific, it carries 20 million tonnes of silt, clay and gravel. Although most of this is carried out to sea, nearly 3.5 million tonnes is dropped along the river valley, creating fertile farmland and an abundance of diverse ecosystems.

The Fraser River is also home to an extraordinarily productive salmon fishery. The area around the mighty Fraser, including the farm land, pulp mills, hydroelectric dams and other commercial undertakings account for 80 percent of British Columbia's GDP.

THE CITY OF VANCOUVER BOASTS

- 1,600 km of paved roads (225 km arterial, 41 km collector, 1,230 km residential, 96 km secondary arterial)
- 18 bridges and viaducts (13 in the city, 5 leading into the city)

DAVID HEWITT'S TOP FIVE MOST ARCHITECTUALLY IMPORTANT VANCOUVER BUILDINGS

David Hewitt is an award winning architect with over 25 years' experience in the business, including 18 years at the helm of Vancouver's Hewitt + Kwasnicky Architects Inc. His numerous accolades and appointments include, among many others, the Aga Khan Foundation Award, the Urban Development Institute and positions on the boards of directors for the Architectural Foundation of BC and the Vancouver International Film Festival.

1. **Museum of Anthropology** at UBC, designed by Arthur Erickson, completed in 1976. This concrete and glass building is Erickson's modern interpretation of the traditional native longhouse. Set on the cliffs above Georgia Strait, the dramatic grand hall opens up to that spectacular setting. The museum houses significant Aboriginal and Asian cultural artifacts.

2. **Marine Building**, Burrard and Hastings Streets, Vancouver, designed by McCarter and Nairne, completed in 1930. This is Vancouver's Art Deco masterpiece. Inspired by the Chrysler Building in New York, the building has been described as a terraced 'wedding cake' with impressive carvings of ships, trains and local sea creatures which signify Vancouver's position as a West Coast sea and rail transportation hub.

- 754 traffic signals (450 full traffic signals, 304 pedestrian actuated signals)
- 56,000 street lights (45,000 road lights, 11,000 lane lights)

Source: City of Vancouver.

3. **Chan Centre for the Performing Arts** at UBC, designed by Bing Thom Architects, completed in 1997. The exterior of the elliptical concert hall is clad with environmentally neutral titanium zinc. Like other Vancouver buildings, the glazed lobby of the Chan opens up to the forest and sea, offering a spectacular yet intimate connection to the West Coast environment.

4. **BC Cancer Research Centre**, Vancouver, designed by IBI / Henriquez Partners, completed in 2003/2004. The recipient of numerous architectural awards, this is also the first health care facility in Canada to be awarded a LEED Gold designation for environmental sustainability. Features include a multi-coloured glazed façade symbolizing a cellular DNA footprint.

5. **Robson Square**, downtown Vancouver, designed by Arthur Erickson, completed in 1970. Robson Square is another of Erickson's masterpieces in Vancouver. Originally commissioned by the provincial government to be a high-rise, Erickson rejected this notion and designed a three block long series of buildings, plazas, waterfalls and indoor malls affectionately referred to as his 'high-rise on its side'. The spectacular seven-story law court building has a massive glazed space frame atrium. The north end is bounded by the historical Vancouver Art Gallery building (the original courthouse building), designed by renowned West Coast architect Francis Rattenbury in 1906.

GETTIN' ROUND

Vancouver's streets form a grid, with named streets running north to south, and avenues, most of which are numbered, running east to west.

You Said Where?

Vancouverites have their own names for city landmarks and communities. Here's a list to help you decipher what those directions mean.

- **Downtown East Side:** This area is the infamous home to one of the poorest neighbourhoods in Canada and is characterized by homelessness, poverty, drug addiction and violence.
- **The Drive:** This is what the locals call Commercial Drive, an ethnically diverse, bohemian east side street.
- **Gastown:** An old part of Vancouver. Originally called Gassy Town, it was named for a steamboat captain turned bartender named 'Gassy' Jack Deighton.
- **Great White Way:** What the locals call Granville Street. It earned the nickname in the 1940s when it was lit up with a sea of bright and artful neon signs. Although the 1970s saw neon fall out of favour, there has been a recent neon sign revival.
- **Kits:** The upscale and hip neighbourhood of Kitsilano, in the west side of the city.
- **PoCo:** Port Coquitlam, one of three cities in Greater Vancouver that includes Coquitlam and Port Moody. Less often used is the term PoCoMo, meaning all three cities.
- **Lower Mainland:** The part of British Columbia that encompasses the Greater Vancouver metropolitan area and the adjacent Fraser Valley.
- **New West:** Refers to New Westminster, an older city that is now part of Greater Vancouver.
- **Royal City:** Another name for New Westminster.

East-West

Broadway (also known as 9th Avenue) is one main unnumbered avenue stretching from the Burnaby boundary in the east end nearly all the way to the University of British Columbia (UBC) campus. King (also known as 25th Avenue), travels parallel to, and 14 blocks south of, Broadway. Hastings Ave. is another major east-to-west thoroughfare. Hastings begins downtown as West Hastings. As it moves east, it turns into — you guessed it — East Hastings, until it reaches Burnaby, when it becomes part of the Burnaby Mountain Parkway and heads to Port Moody.

North-South

Important north-to-south streets include Burrard, which begins downtown at Canada Place and makes its way through the city core before heading south across False Creek (hello, Burrard Street Bridge) to West 16th. Commercial Drive, which also stretches from the Burrard Inlet to West 16th, is home to one of the city's most ethnically diverse and alternative areas. Boundary, another north-south street, runs from the inlet to the Fraser River and — not surprisingly, given its name — acts as the boundary between Vancouver and Burnaby.

Did you know...

that streets in downtown Vancouver are 66 feet wide and blocks are 450 feet long?

Did you know...

that St. James Anglican Church was built in 1927 with the assistance of Sir Adrian Gilbert Scott, the lesser known brother of Sir Giles Gilbert Scott, the man responsible for the classic red British phone booth?

"Lord Stanley threw his arms to the heavens, as though embracing within them the whole of one thousand acres of primeval forest, and dedicated it 'to the use and enjoyment of peoples of all colours, creeds, and customs, for all time.'"
— An observer writing about the official opening of Stanley Park.

COMMUNITIES

Greater Vancouver is home to 23 different communities. Residential districts include Strathcona in the east end, Victoria-Fraserview going from East 41st to the Fraser River and Kerrisdale in the city's southwest.

Commercial areas include the downtown core, Oakridge located in the central part of the city and defined by a number of busy streets, Gastown with its trendy restaurants and art galleries (and its famous steam clock), and Fairview on the south side of False Creek, home to the city's hospitals and several shopping malls and boutiques.

As in most cities, a large socio-economic gap divides Vancouver's affluent neighbourhoods, such as Shaughnessy and Yaletown, and the poorer ones, such as Dickens and Hastings-Sunrise. This gap is especially obvious at the nexus between the Downtown core and the Downtown East Side.

Sources: City of Vancouver; BC PassPort; Straight.com; Statistics Canada.

Did you know...

that the Sam Kee Building at 8 West Pender Street is reportedly the thinnest office building in the world? It is just under 1.5 metres wide.

They Said It

"In New York you get pigeons, in Vancouver there are eagles; you don't see little herring swimming in Vancouver, you see giant Orcas. It's all so spectacular!"
— Actor Isabella Rossellini in an interview with *Weekly Scoop* Magazine.

The Grand Old Man

Arthur Charles Erickson, at 84, is now the 'grand old man' of Canadian architecture with a worldwide reputation. Born and raised in Vancouver, he began his study at UBC in languages before going to McGill to study architecture.

Almost fresh out of school, Erickson won a competition that essentially gave him free reign to design Simon Fraser University in Burnaby. Soon he was designing buildings around the globe, some of which include the California Plaza in Los Angeles, the Museum of Glass in Tacoma, the Canadian Embassy in Washington and the Napp Laboratories in England.

Although Erickson still travels extensively, Vancouver is his home and his architectural footprint can be seen everywhere. The Museum of Anthropology at UBC is an Erickson creation, as is Robson Square, the modern civic centre and public plaza, located in the downtown, the private residence called the Graham House, the Waterfall Building, MacMillan Bloedel tower on Georgia Street and the list goes on.

Erickson's designed buildings are modernist and take into account natural conditions, including climate and location. He was particularly influenced by Frank Lloyd Wright and is a firm proponent on the importance of "feeling," not thinking, in design. Although he has been called the concrete poet (he calls concrete the marble of the 20th century), he refuses to be pigeonholed by a particular school. His work at the Museum of Anthropology in Vancouver is an example of that, drawing in that case on the inspiration provided by the post and beam architecture of the West Coast First Nations.

Erickson remains a vibrant and prolific member of the global architectural community. In Vancouver he is proudly and affectionately known as "Arthur." He currently heads up the Arthur Erickson Architectural Corporation.

TREE INVENTORY

- Value of trees lining Vancouver streets: $500 million
- Number of trees lining streets: 130,000
- Number of species: 600
- Number planted in the past decade: 40,000

Source: Vancouver Board of Parks and Recreation.

BRANCHING OUT

Vancouver takes its trees very seriously, even dictating how they must be treated. Vancouver homeowners are allowed to cut down only one tree a year from their properties. That tree should be more than 20 cm wide and to cut it they'll need both a permit and a new one, which must be planted to replace every felled tree.

PARKS

About 1,300 hectares — or 11 percent — of Vancouver's area is reserved for and preserved as parkland. The city proper is home to 221 parks, which range in size from the 400-hectare Stanley Park to a tiny, unnamed park in the east end.

BEACHES

Vancouver has nine beaches open to the public, with lifeguards on duty from Victoria Day until Labour Day. They include eight expan-

Take 5 TOP FIVE MOST VISITED
BEACHES (VISITS, 2006)

1. **Second Beach:** 673,825
2. **English Bay:** 422,280
3. **Kitsilano Beach:** 387,445
4. **Locarno Beach:** 347,415
5. **Third Beach:** 333,781

Source: Vancouver Parks and Recreation.

sive ocean-side locations: English Bay, Jericho, Kitsilano, Locarno, Second Beach, Spanish Bank, Sunset, and Third Beach and one fresh-water beach at Trout Lake. The average ocean water temperatures usually range from about 14°C in May to 20°C in August. In 2006, the beaches drew more than 3.3 million visitors.

Source: City of Vancouver.

ECOLOGICAL FOOTPRINTS

An ecological footprint measures how much land and water a human population needs to produce what it consumes and to absorb its waste.

- Average number of hectares used to sustain a Canadian, or their "ecological footprints": 7.25
- Montrealer: 6.89
- Vancouverite: 7.31
- Torontonian: 7.36
- Calgarian: 9.86

Sources: Global Foot Print Network; Federation of Canadian Municipalities.

Did you know...

that Vancouver's largest tree is a giant sequoia whose trunk circumference measures over 18 ft? It is located on Cambie Street near King Edward.

PLAY IT AGAIN!

- 400 playing fields and sports courts
- 150 playground structures
- 200 tennis courts
- 17.5 km of beaches
- 15 indoor and outdoor pools
- 8 ice rinks
- 3 public full-length golf courses
- 3 public pitch-n-putt golf courses

Source: Vancouver Park Board.

Granville Makeover

Almost 125 years ago, a modest wooden bridge crossed False Creek joining two ends of Granville Street. Beneath the span were two sandbars, the long-used fishing grounds of Aboriginal people.

In 1915, Vancouver officials hatched plans for this sandbar they christened "Industrial Island." They spent $342,000 scooping mud and rock from around False Creek, creating a foundation upon which forest, mining, construction and shipping industries were built.

The progress of the project fluctuated. The Great Depression scuttled it, World War 2 revived it, and by the 1950s the fortunes of Granville Island were again sagging. By then, its years as an industrial site had turned False Creek into a bay of toxic sledge. Cost thwarted plans to fill in the remainder of the Creek to create more industrial land, so just a few acres were added, turning the one-time island into a peninsula.

New plans for Granville Island were born in the 1970s by planners with innovative ideas—they set about building a people-friendly space in the bustling city and they succeeded. Today Granville Island is an urban oasis home to fresh food markets, restaurants, theatres, art galleries and studios that attract 12 million visitors each year.

URBAN TRANSPORTATION

The 1,800 km^2 Vancouver transit system includes buses, trollies, a rapid transit system and ferries. The South Coast British Columbia Transportation Authority (TransLink) and the Metro Vancouver transportation authority are responsible for public transportation. Standard fares are $2.50 for an adult and $1.75 for a child.

BUS/TROLLIES

Standard and rapid buses; emission-free electric trollies.

- 180 routes
- 8,000 bus stops

SKYTRAIN

- 49 km of track, starting at the Vancouver waterfront
- 32 stations
- 210 railcars
- 200,000 passengers per day

SEABUS FERRIES

Traverse the Burrard Inlet between downtown and North Vancouver.

- 2 ferries
- Serves 16,000 passengers each weekday
- Crossing: Less than 13 minutes
- Reliability: 99.9 percent scheduled sailings made

Did you know...

that the George Massey Tunnel in Greater Vancouver that connects Richmond and Delta is the lowest portion of road below sea level in all of Canada?

Take 5 VANCOUVER'S TALLEST BUILDINGS

1. **Living Shangri La**	201 m
2. **One Wall Centre**	150 m
3. **Shaw Tower**	149 m
4. **Harbour Centre** (no antenna)	146 m
5. **Granville Square**	138 m

Source: Emporis Corporation.

WEST COAST EXPRESS

Commuter rail service linking Mission, Maple Ridge, Pitt Meadows, Port Moody, Port Coquitlam and Coquitlam with downtown Vancouver.

- 65 km
- 8 stations
- Travel time: 73 minutes, one way
- Frequency: every 30 minutes (approximately)
- 7,700 passengers per day

ALBION CAR FERRY

Two ferries connect Maple Ridge and Pitt Meadows on the north side of the Fraser River to Langley and Surrey on the south side.

- Fare: Free
- The Albion Ferry is expected to be replaced by the Golden Ears Bridge in late 2008.

Sources: TransLink; Greater Vancouver Transportation Authority.

Did you know...

that almost 3 million ladybugs are released annually to control aphid infestations on street trees?

They Said It

"Whenever we witness art in a building, we are aware of an energy contained by it."

– Vancouver Architect, Arthur Erickson.

EYE OF THE LION

Interested in the economic potential of West Vancouver, the Irish Guinness family (yes, the famed brewers) built the First Narrow's Bridge, better known as the Lions Gate Bridge, across Burrard Inlet. The 472 m long, 61.0 m high bridge opened in 1938. For a quarter century the Guinness family collected the tolls but in 1963 the province purchased the bridge for $6 million and removed the tolls. The Guinness family was still proud of its contribution to the city, though, and to mark Expo '86, the family had lights installed on the bridge as a gift.

DOWNTOWN

Downtown Vancouver is home to retail, entertainment venues and sports stadiums which attract locals and tourists alike. Nearly 4,000 hotel rooms have been added to the downtown since 1985 and new residential areas are also booming there. During the 1990s alone, the population of the downtown peninsula increased by more than 20,000, reaching 70,000. This makes Vancouver's downtown the fastest growing in North America. The trend is expected to continue — by 2021 40,000 more people will live downtown.

Sources: Metro Vancouver; Avison Young.

GETTING DOWNTOWN

- 40 percent take the bus
- 39 percent drive
- 27 percent walk
- 3 percent cycle

Source: Statistics Canada.

IT ALL HAPPENS ON ROBSON

In the heart of Vancouver's downtown is Robson Street, a bustling hub of shopping and eating. Named after John Robson, Premier of British Columbia from 1889 to 1892, Robson has been the centre of attention since train tracks lined its streets in 1895. Today, Robson Street is prime shopping territory as it is lined with more than 176 shops. With average rents of $208 per square foot, it is one of the most expensive places in the country to open a business and so, not surprisingly, stores here tend to be high end.

Source: Robson Street Business Association.

WASTING AWAY

Metro Vancouver generates more than three million tonnes of waste — that's about 0.69 tonnes per person.

Waste	Generated (tonnes)	Recycled (Percentage)
Residential	821,092	44.8
Institutional/ Commercial and Light-industrial	1.06 million	38.1
Demolition, Land Clearing and Construction	1.07 million	65.5
Product Stewardship	122,413	100

Source: Greater Vancouver Regional District.

Did you know...

that the Stanley Park Rose Garden, first planted in 1920 by the Kiwanis Club, now boasts more than 3,500 plants annually?

Weblinks

City Lights: Vancouver's Neon Heritage

epe.lac-bac.gc.ca/100/205/301/ic/cdc/neon/main.html

This site hosts scenes of Vancouver's neon past, images and information compiled by the Vancouver Museum, a true example of the city's 'urban geography'.

Heritage Vancouver Society

heritagevancouver.org

Heritage Vancouver is a group that aims to preserve the city's heritage buildings and historic landscapes.

Interactive Map

map.mapnetwork.com/destination/vancouver/

Check out this very cool, very useful, map of Vancouver, courtesy of Tourism Vancouver.

Did you know...

that Vancouver is the only city of its size on the continent without a single freeway?

Did you know...

that more than 50,000 dogs live in the city? There are 31 dog-off-leash sites in Vancouver.

Weather and Climate

Surrounded by water on three sides and by the Coast Range mountains on the other, Vancouver's climate is moderated by ocean current and protected from the continental freezes by the Rocky Mountains. As a result, it has one of the mildest climates in Canada. Temperatures average 3°C in January and 18°C in July. Vancouver's average annual precipitation is 1,219 mm. The temperature is mild enough that the city's Parks Board has planted palm trees.

The biggest differences between seasons in Vancouver lie in total sunshine and rainfall amounts. Summertime sees far more sun and less rain, while winter months, though short on snow, are very rainy. On those rare occasions when snow does fall, it melts quickly.

Vancouver's reputation as a particularly rainy city is only partly deserved. True, the winter months can be extremely wet and it is not uncommon to get 20 consecutive days or more with some rain. In summer months, however, Vancouver's rainfall is not extraordinary—even Toronto gets more rain at that time of year.

DAILY AVERAGE TEMPERATURES (°C)

Jan	Feb	Mar	Apr	May	Jun	Jul	Aug	Sep	Oct	Nov	Dec
3.3	4.8	6.6	9.2	12.5	15.2	17.5	17.6	14.6	10.1	6.0	3.5

They Said It

WEATHER AT A GLANCE

- Rainiest month: January, 139.1 mm
- Least rainy month: August, 39.1 mm
- Snowiest month: January, 16.6 cm
- Month with greatest snow depth: January and February, average of 1 cm of snow
- Windiest month: March, winds 12.9 km/h
- Sunniest month: July, 294.5 hours of bright sunshine

Source: Environment Canada.

WEATHER WINNERS

- Record high: 33.3°C on August 9, 1960
- Record low: -17.8°C on January 14, 1950
- Record rainfall in one day: 89.4 mm on December 25, 1972
- Record snowfall in one day: 41 cm, on December 29, 1996
- Record wind gust: 129 km/h on November 25, 1957
- Record daily sustained wind: 89 km/h on February 20, 1960
- Record wind chill: -27.8°C on December 16, 1964
- Record humidex: 37.9°C on July 28, 1998

Source: Environment Canada.

RAIN CITY

Vancouver gets more than its fair share of rain thanks to a meteorological phenomenon that is commonly referred to as the Pineapple Express. Moisture and subsequent heavy rainfall from waters associated with the Hawaiian Islands are driven north to Vancouver by a Pacific jet stream. Vancouver ranks ninth among Canadian cities when it comes to rainfall, logging 1,154.7 mm a year. By comparison, Canada's two rainiest cities are Prince Rupert (2,468.5 mm) and Port Alberni (1,797.94 mm) and the least rainy cities are Whitehorse (163.13 mm) and Yellowknife (164.5 mm).

Source: Environment Canada; The Weather Notebook.

Rising Waters

Vancouver-area residents are no strangers to sandbags thanks in large part to the mighty Fraser River flowing past their city. The Fraser is known to spill its banks in the spring if the Rocky Mountain snow pack melts too quickly.

The year 1894 saw the worst recorded flood, but because the human population at that time was small, the measurable damage was slight. In 1948, however, the Fraser flooded again, this time displacing more than 16,000 residents, forcing business closures and washing out roads. The '48 flood cost the area $20 million dollars, or about $150 million in today's money.

The next big flood happened in 1972. Fortunately, improved dyking prevented a repeat of the crisis of '48. Still, the damage was significant and, when all was said and done, the cleanup cost $10 million, or $37 million at today's prices.

The 300,000 people living on the lower Fraser floodplain are mindful of The Big One — a massive flood; the likes of which are expected to happen once each century. The 1948 flood is considered one such "One Hundred Year Flood," and scientists predict that that there is a 1 in 3 chance that a flood of that magnitude will occur in the next fifty years.

In 2007, those on the Fraser's floodplain breathed a collective sigh of relief when dire flood predictions failed to materialize.

Take 5 MARK MADRYGA'S TOP FIVE
VANCOUVER WEATHER EVENTS

Mark Madryga is an Environment Canada Certified Meteorologist and an operational forecaster with Environment Canada at the Pacific Storm Prediction Centre in Vancouver. He also brings Vancouverites their weather news on Global Television and CKNW AM Radio 980. These are his picks for top weather stories.

1. The Stanley Park Windstorm, December 15th, 2006: Likely the highest profile storm in Vancouver's history, it was, unbelievably, the third vicious windstorm to hit the city in five days. Storms on the previous Monday and Wednesday generated severe wind, leaving nearly 200,000 people on the South Coast without power. The most powerful storm of the three arrived in the Vancouver area early Friday morning. Between 3 and 4 am, a blast of westerly wind swept into English Bay and took aim at Stanley Park. Thousands of trees, an estimated 20 percent of all the trees in the park, were uprooted or broken. Landslides caused by the storm undermined the seawall around Stanley Park, closing the popular walking and jogging route for months.

2. Typhoon Freda, October 12th, 1962: Many Vancouverites recall this storm as if it happened yesterday. Freda, born ten days earlier west of the International Dateline, weakened somewhat before approaching North America's West Coast. Northern California, then Oregon felt its impact, with one station reporting a wind gust of over 280 km/h. The storm struck Vancouver early on Saturday, October 12th, with peak wind gusts at Vancouver International Airport of 126 km/h and up to 145 km/h in the Fraser Valley. Vancouver felt the storm's fury for four hours. In Stanley Park, trees were leveled, power outages were felt by half of all residents and seven deaths were attributed to the storm.

3. The Snowstorm of December 29th, 1996: Frigid arctic air settled over southern BC between December 23rd and the 29th, the day on which a vigorous Pacific storm deposited heavy snow across the region. Victoria and the eastern Vancouver Island were hit the hardest, with between 60 and 100 cm burying most areas. The 44 cm recorded at Vancouver Airport paralyzed the city (thankfully it was a Sunday) and cancelled events and ferry runs, preventing many from getting anywhere. The storm generated more than 500 avalanches and cost approximately $200 million.

4. **The Wettest Month and the Boil Water Advisory, November 2006:** This phenomenal month of storms began with five straight days of rainfall totaling over 130 mm. By month's end, 351 mm of precipitation had fallen, equaling the wettest November on record. But it was the storm of mid-month that had the most impact. Severe rainfall on November 16th led to water quality warnings affecting more than two million people living in the Greater Vancouver region. As the storm triggered landslides in the region's three water reservoirs, sediment levels raised to levels that were ninety times higher than those permitted under federal standards. A boil water warning was issued and the region's Chief Medical Health Officer advised that tap water not be used at all. Restaurants had to stop serving many food products and many of Vancouver's coffee shops were closed.

5. **The Incredible Winter Storm, January 20th, 1935:** On January 19th, the temperature at the Jericho Beach weather station fell to -17°C. The next day, a massive storm blanketed the Lower Mainland in 45 cm of snow, closing mills, schools, and businesses and paralyzing traffic. Three to four foot snowdrifts (up to 120 cm) led to streetcars being upended. If that weren't enough, milder air swept in later that day, depositing an additional 30 mm of rain on top of the heavy wet snow. Over the next four days, Vancouver recorded an additional 230 mm of rain which resulted in flood waters likely never seen before in the city. Roofs succumbed to the tremendous weight of wet snow, including that of the PNE Forum, the city's hockey and curling rink. Communications wires also collapsed, cutting Vancouver off from direct contact with the east.

HIGHS AND LOWS: VANCOUVER WEATHER TERMS

Pineapple Express: A sub-tropical air mass from Hawaii that brings warm air and an abundance of moisture to the BC coast.

An Outflow: A wind pattern where air from the mainland interior is drawn out. It means that in the winter the coldest of airs are coming, and in the summer it means to expect the hottest winds.

An Aleutian Low: The semi-permanent low-pressure area that sits in the Gulf of Alaska during the winter months and directs frontal systems towards Vancouver, sometimes bringing heavy rains.

A Hawaiian High: It's not a special brand of BC bud, but rather a high-pressure area that builds off the West Coast in the summer, producing dry, sunny weather.

COOL SUMMERS

Vancouver is one of Canada's coolest cities in the summertime. In a list of the country's 100 mildest communities ordered according to temperatures reached during the summer, Vancouver ranks 91st. The city's highest average afternoon temperature in June, July and August is 20.9°C, similar to other coastal cities including Fort St. John's on the West Coast and Corner Brook, Newfoundland and Labrador. In contrast, Kamloops, BC, has the hottest summers in Canada, with mercury topping out at an average of 27°C and Prince Rupert, BC, the chilliest with a cool daily summertime average of 16°C.

They Said It

> "It's odd. People here in Vancouver tend to complain about the rain and overcast conditions. HELLO?! Have you lived in Winnipeg? How about Regina or Edmonton? They deal with brown, dry, dirty weather. We're blessed with lush, moist, snow free, green surroundings. Get over it!"
>
> – Jonny Staub, Midday Personality,
> The Beat 94.5 FM (CFBT FM) Vancouver.

AVERAGE FEBRUARY TEMPERATURES
IN FIVE NORTH AMERICAN CITIES

1. **Montreal:** -8.4°C
2. **New York:** 0.9°C
3. **Chicago:** -3.7°C
4. **Los Angeles:** 14.2°C
5. **Vancouver:** 4.8°C

Sources: Cityrating.com; Environment Canada.

DESPARATELY SEEKING THE SUN

Vancouver is not the place for die-hard sun-seekers. Out of 100 Canadian cities, Vancouver finishes 25th when it comes to the fewest number of sunny days each year. The sun makes an appearance in Vancouver on 288.4 days each year — more often than it does in Prince Rupert, BC (250.2 days, the nation's least sunny) and St. John's, NL (270.3 days), but considerably less often than in Calgary (332.9 days, the nation's sunniest) or Winnipeg (317.7 days).

Source: Environment Canada.

GREY SKIES

The tenth cloudiest city in Canada, Vancouver is overcast for 5,214 hours each year. Compare that to Prince Rupert — the country's cloudiest — which records 6,145.7 cloudy hours a year, and Swift Current — the country's least cloudy — which records an enviable 3,840.6 hours of cloud cover each year.

They Said It

"Vancouver rain, Vancouver rain,
Again I hear its soft refrain
Tap-tapping on the windowpane."
— **Robert Service** in *Harper of Heaven:*
A Further Adventure into Memory.

Take 5 — AVERAGE YEARLY RAINFALL

FOR FIVE CANADIAN CITIES (RANKING OUT OF 100 CANADIAN PLACES IN AVERAGE RAINFALL)

1. **Halifax**, 1,254.3 mm (6)
2. **Vancouver**, 1,154.7 (9)
3. **Montreal**, 760.0 (45)
4. **Toronto**, 684.6 (58)
5. **Saskatoon**, 265.2 (95)

Source: Statistics Canada.

GROWING SEASON

The growing season often begins in February and continues until October. Summers are variable, some with several consecutive days of heavy rains and others that don't see rain for five weeks or more at a time. During the latter, un-watered grass may not need to be cut for over a month.

Source: Environment Canada.

DELIGHTFULLY WARM

Vancouver is the second warmest city in the country with an annual average low temperature 10.1°C. Only Chilliwack's average low of 10.5°C is warmer. Comparatively, Yellowknife, Canada's coldest city, has an annual temperature of -4.6°C. Vancouver also has the fewest freezing days of any city in the country, with the mercury dipping below zero fewer than 46 days a year. Victoria and Chilliwack are not far behind with 52.6 and 54.4 days respectively while the two cities with the most below-freezing days are Thompson with 239.85 days and Whitehorse with 225 days.

Source: Environment Canada.

They Said It

"Did you hear about the Vancouver Rain Festival? It runs from September 1st to August 31st."
  – An Anonymous jokester, down on Vancouver's weather reputation.

They Said It

"No where else in Canada can you jog in shorts in February, but also sometimes see your breath in July. The great thing about Vancouver is, no matter what the weather is like, we're always outside enjoying it."

– Graham Hatch, ROCK 101 Radio.

SLIGHT SNOW

By Canadian standards, Vancouver's annual snowfall is slight. Out of Canada's 100 snowiest cities, Vancouver finished 98th, with an annual total snowfall of just 48.17 cm, more than only fellow West Coast towns, Duncan (46.11 cm) and Victoria (43.7 cm). This is a far cry from Gander, Canada's snowiest city, where 443.13 cm fall each year.

LAMENT OF THE SNOW SHOVEL

Few Vancouverites own snow shovels and this makes sense given that the city is one of the least snowy in Canada. The city just has 10.9 days a year with snowfall of 0.2 cm or more, a far cry from Val d'Or's 103.5 days and pretty far off the snowfalls of other cities such as St. John's (84.2 days), Montreal (60.4 days), Calgary (56.8 days) and Toronto (46.5 days). When it does fall, Vancouver's white stuff is wet and, if it doesn't melt immediately, can make for very slippery road conditions. Unaccustomed to winter driving, this is probably the reason behind the perception that Vancouverites are collectively unable to drive in the snow.

Source: Environment Canada.

Did you know...

that the Vancouver Folk Music Festival, an outdoor music festival held over two days and three evenings, chooses to hold its event on the third weekend of July each year because that is when it is historically least likely to rain in the summer?

Garden City

Blessed with the longest growing season in the country, Vancouver is a city of gardens and gardeners. Fertile soil and mild weather simply allow for horticultural diversity that is not available in most of Canada.

Stanley Park is the city's green jewel but is also home to the Rose Garden and Shakespeare Garden. A recent addition to the park's garden is the community garden, a section of park reserved for 30 plots of flower gardens tended by volunteer residents of the city.

The city's public garden resides in Queen Elizabeth Park; the park includes fountains, statues (including one by sculptor Henry Moore), flower gardens and an arboretum featuring all Canadian tree species. It is also home to the Bloedel Floral Conservatory, a dome bursting with exotic plants, tropical flowers, birds and Koi fish.

Several Vancouver gardens reflect the city's ethnic composition with Asian gardening practices figuring prominently. UBC botanical gardens consist of seventy acres of 10,000 different flowers, shrubs and trees. The famous Japanese Nitobe Gardens, a traditional Japanese "Tea and Stroll" garden, is regarded as one of best outside of Japan. The Dr. Sun Yat Sen Classical Chinese Garden, which opened on the edge of Chinatown in 1986, is one of the first of its kind outside of China. Named after the "Father of Modern China," the garden boasts the four main elements of a classical Chinese garden: rock, water, plants, and architecture.

Other gardens include those at Tilford Park, which boasts 24 varieties of roses and manicured Bonsai bamboo trees, the 22-acre Van Dusen Botanical Garden with its notable Elizabethan hedge maze and Minster Park's 27-acre collection of 11 theme gardens.

April and May are the busiest months for gardeners. The University of British Columbia Botanical Garden has the city's largest annual plant sales on Mother's Day every year. The Vancouver Park Board also opens a number of private gardens to the public for a weekend in spring during its annual garden tour.

They Said It

"The fact that I'm playing in a Canadian market, the beauty of Vancouver with its incredible weather and things to do, that's just icing on the cake."
— **Anson Carter on playing hockey in Vancouver.**

DREAMING OF A WHITE CHRISTMAS

Vancouver has just an 11 percent chance of snowy weather on December 25, pretty poor odds compared to the 100 percent chance of Goose Bay, Quebec City and Timmins. In fact, Vancouver and Victoria tie for the Canadian cities with the least chance of a White Christmas. Vancouver had a white Christmas in 2007 but, in typical Vancouver fashion, it was wet snow that turned to rain. On that odds-beating day, one centimetre of snow fell at Vancouver International Airport. The greatest snowfall recorded for a Vancouver Christmas Day was 17.5 cm in 1971.

Source: Environment Canada.

PAYING FOR WINTER

Each year Vancouver allots $750,000 for snow removal, though additional contingency funds are available. Given the infrequency of snowfall in the city, no city employees are assigned snow removal duties only but as many as 35 truck drivers are available for snow removal duties on streets as required and 51 city trucks can be outfitted with ploughs and salting machines to handle winter roads.

Source: City of Vancouver Streets Department.

Did you know...

that Grouse Mountain ski resort, which looms in Vancouver's scenic backdrop, makes 75 percent of its snow on average because of the lack of winter snowfall?

WIND

Vancouver is in the lower half of windy cities in Canada, ranking 59th. Each year, Vancouver gets 16.6 days on which winds gust for at least one hour at speeds of 40 km/hr. This compares to St. John's, Canada's windiest city, which boasts 127.1 such days. Vancouver's highest average hourly speed annually is 11.8 km/hr.

THUNDERSTORMS

Vancouver has a low incidence of thunderstorms. On average, there are 6.1 days each year on which a thunderstorm occurs. Nanaimo has the lowest of any Canadian centre with only 2.3 days, while Windsor, Ontario has the highest with 33.2. By way of comparison, the thunder claps through the skies over Toronto during 27.9 days per year, in Calgary 27.3 days, in Montreal 24.4 days and in Halifax 11.3 days.

Source: Environment Canada.

Take 5 TOP FIVE WINTER ACTIVITIES
IN VANCOUVER

1. **Ski:** There are plenty of ski resorts nearby, including Grouse, Cypress and Seymour Mountains. A little further away are Whistler and Blackcomb Mountains.
2. **Sail:** Some of the best sailing times happen during winter months because of the wind and because Vancouver's mild weather makes sailing possible most of the year.
3. **Golf:** Most of Vancouver's golf clubs operate year round. It's true that Vancouverites can ski in the morning and golf in the afternoon.
4. **Tennis:** On those occasions when winter weather produces a dry spell, Vancouver's tennis courts get busy.
5. **Swim:** The odd hardy person is known to venture into Vancouver's outdoor swimming areas for a quick dip and on the January 1st Polar Bear Swim thousands of people fearlessly wade into the Pacific.

Weblinks

Environment Canada, Weather Winners

www.on.ec.gc.ca/weather/winners/intro-e.html

In a war of weather between Canada's major cities, see how Vancouver stacks up!

Weather Cam

www.westinbayshore.com/cam/index.php

This website maintained by the Westin Bayshore hotel is trained on coastal downtown Vancouver. This site will show you Vancouver's weather conditions, in real time.

Earthquake!

Scientists agree that Vancouver's southern BC home is overdue for a big quake. Located in an active earthquake zone along a 1,400 km fault line, no major jolt has shaken the ground for more than a half century.

This is not to say that Vancouver has been earthquake free — about 3,000 mild tremors occur each year. Scientists predict two scenarios. A moderate quake, 6-7 on the Richtcer Scale, is most likely and would cause considerable damage and deaths.

Less likely is a massive quake registering 8.5 or more on the Richter Scale. In this case, damage would be severe: up to 30 percent of Vancouver homes would be damaged, up to 100 percent of older masonry buildings would collapse and 15 percent of high rises might be uninhabitable. The airport would suffer damage, water systems would fail, 45 percent of schools would collapse and deaths would measure in the thousands.

Vancouver is, however, preparing. Emergency response teams are in place and structures in the city have been upgraded to increase the odds of their surviving a quake of such magnitude.

People

Vancouver has always been a city of immigrants and neighbourhoods. Unlike other Canadian cities, whose initial cultural makeup consisted largely of Europeans with small enclaves of Africans and First Nations people, Vancouver's position on the Pacific Rim made it a destination for immigrants not typically attracted to Canadian centres.

As early as 1869, the young town of Granville was already home to significant Chinese and Japanese populations, brought here by the gold rush, the Pacific fishery and the construction of the railway. Today, 831,265 residents, or almost 40 percent of the population, were born outside the country.

Asian immigration to Vancouver ebbed and flowed throughout its history, slowed at times by racist federal immigration policy and laws of exclusion. A resurgence of immigration from Asia in the latter part of the 20th century has had a profound influence on the city. When displaced Hong Kongers sought to escape the Chinese takeover, the Chinese displaced the German and Irish as the single largest non-Anglo ethnic group in the city.

The city has benefited from the waves of immigration. Early in the twentieth century, Germans made their mark on the city. After WWII they were joined by others, notably Italians, Greeks, Indians, Vietnamese, Filipinos, Koreans, Africans and South Americans. Together they have made Vancouver the city in North America with

They Said It

the second highest proportion of foreign-born citizens.

It's not always been a smooth road, but today Vancouver embraces
its ethnic diversity. Shop and restaurant signs written in many languages dot the cityscape. In some areas of the city, notably in
Chinatown and the Punjabi Market, street signs appear in English as
well as in the mother tongues of community residents. City government has taken to using diversity to attract business.

The city publishes municipal documents and offers services in several languages. There is also increasing interaction between communities. For example, 7.2 percent of married or common law couples in
Vancouver are interracial — more than double the Canadian average
of 3.2 percent, and greater than the rates in either Toronto (6.1 percent) or Montreal (3.5 percent).

FOREIGN BORN RESIDENTS AS A PERCENTAGE OF TOTAL POPULATION

A Comparison of Selected Metropolitan Centres

- Toronto: 45.7
- **Vancouver: 39.6**
- Los Angeles: 34.7
- New York City: 27.9
- Montreal: 20.6

Source: The Sustainable Region Initiative.

Did you know...

that 826,935 Vancouverites are first generation Canadians?

Mr. Green

David Takayoshi Suzuki was born in Vancouver (with his twin sister Marcia) in 1936. The young Suzuki was a third-generation Japanese Canadian. During the World War II, however, for Japanese Canadians it didn't matter how many generations families had been in Canada.

In 1942, the government sold the family's Marpole area dry cleaning business and sent Suzuki's father to a labour camp in Solsqua. Suzuki, his pregnant mother and two sisters were sent to another camp at Slocan in the British Columbia Interior.

After the war, the Suzuki family moved east to Ontario, eventually settling in London. He would win a scholarship to Amherst College in Massachusetts, graduating with an Honours B.A. in Biology in 1958 and he would graduate with a PhD in zoology from the University of Chicago in 1961.

Suzuki would return home to the West Coast and Vancouver in 1963, this time for good. He worked as a professor at the University of British Columbia from his arrival until he retired in 2001. (He continues as professor emeritus with UBC's Sustainable Development Research Institute.)

Suzuki began to do some work in the mainstream media as early as 1969. In the early 1970s, he had his own show with CBC. He did well enough there that in 1979, CBC offered him the job of host of a new television show called *The Nature of Things*. The show didn't dumb down science but rather made it accessible. The show, if anything, has become more relevant in an increasing specialized world.

Today, *The Nature of Things* is not only seen in Canada but in more than 50 countries around the world. In a countrywide content, Canadians named Suzuki one of the six most important Canadians in history. Although into his early seventies now, Suzuki is still an important force and advocate in Canadian and world environmental issues. He established the David Suzuki Foundation in 1990 to find ways for society to live in balance with the natural world. American environmentalist and writer Bill McKibben calls him one of a handful of the most important environmental thinkers in the world.

ETHNIC ORIGIN OF VANCOUVERITES (CMA, INCLUDES MULTIPLE RESPONSES, 2006)

- British Isles   35.9 percent
- East and South East Asian   27.9 percent
- Western European   13.8 percent
- South Asian   9.9 percent
- Southern European   8.2 percent
- French   6.6 percent
- Northern European   5.9 percent

Take 5 ELDON YELLOWHORN'S FIVE ISSUES
FACING VANCOUVER'S ABORIGINAL COMMUNITY

Eldon Yellowhorn is from Alberta's Piikani First Nation but has lived in Vancouver for over ten years. He is an Associate Professor in the Department of Archaeology and director of the First Nations Studies program at Simon Fraser University and co-author of *First Peoples in Canada*. Vancouver is home to BC's largest aboriginal community.

1. **Building a community:** A new generation of Aboriginal people knows only urban life. For them, defining new traditions and deciding what customs to celebrate and modify will be paramount. Urban Aboriginal communities might never occupy a formal space (as do Chinatown or Little India) but they can imagine a community driven by a common purpose.

2. **Finding a voice:** Removed from band councils and federal politics (where Aboriginal politicians typically focus), Vancouver's Aboriginal population does not yet influence Vancouver politics. A new urban political class must champion Aboriginal issues by appealing to the general electorate (Vancouverites do not cast ballots in civic electoral districts — top candidates form city council).

- Aboriginal — 2.8 percent
- North American Indian — 2.1 percent
- West Asian — 1.9 percent
- Latin/Central/South American — 1.4 percent
- African — 1.1 percent
- Oceania origins — 8.6 percent
- Arab — 6.8 percent
- Caribbean — 5.6 percent
- Pacific Islands origins — 5.0 percent

Source: Statistics Canada.

3. **Growing the Aboriginal middle class:** Aboriginals lack the training needed to share in Vancouver's wealth. Growing the Aboriginal middle class begins with ensuring Aboriginal educational success rates on par with those of the general population. This will benefit the entire community and lead urban Aboriginals away from poverty.

4. **Improving quality of life:** Health is the best measure for quality of life. Aboriginals who suffer disproportionate to their numbers fare poorly in this measure. Promotion of healthy lifestyles will inject confidence in other facets of personal and social interactions.

5. **Fostering a positive youth culture:** The youth who dominate Vancouver's Aboriginal population lack economic and political power and rely on their elders as advocates. As they enter adulthood, their influence on twenty-first century civic life will be as significant as that of the "baby boom" on the twentieth century. Adults must ensure that youth grow into strong citizens of Vancouver.

Take 5 — TOP FIVE LANGUAGES
USED IN VANCOUVER

1. **English**
2. **Chinese** (includes Cantonese and Mandarin)
3. **French**
4. **Punjabi**
5. **Hindi**

Source: Vancouver Economic Development.

IMMIGRANT POPULATION IN METRO VANCOUVER

	2006	1996	1986
Total Pop.	2,097,960	1,813,935	1,362,025
Immigrant Pop.	831,265	633,745	391,515
As a Proportion of Total	40 percent	35 percent	29 percent

Source: The Sustainable Region Initiative.

PLACE OF BIRTH OF IMMIGRANTS TO METRO VANCOUVER

Country of Origin	No. Total Immigrants	As a Percentage
Asia (includes Middle East)	543,255	65
China	137,245	17
Hong Kong	75,780	9
Philippines	62,960	8
India	90,095	11
Europe	182,150	22
Northern Europe	73,435	9
Western Europe	31,740	4
Eastern Europe	40,420	5
Southern Europe	36,550	4
Africa	27,260	3
United States	24,780	3
Oceania and other	24,090	3

Source: The Sustainable Region Initiative.

FOREIGN BORN RESIDENTS AS A PROPORTION OF MUNICIPAL POPULATION

Municipality	As a Percentage
Anmore	16
Belcarra	22
Bowen Island	25
Burnaby	51
Coquitlam	39
Delta	28
Electoral Area 'A'	47
Langley City	18
Langley Township	17
Lions Bay	27
Maple Ridge	17
New Westminster	32
North Vancouver City	37
North Vancouver District	32
Pitt Meadows	21
Port Coquitlam	28
Port Moody	29
Richmond	57
Surrey	38
Vancouver	46
West Vancouver	37
White Rock	24

Source: The Sustainable Region Initiative.

Did you know...

that by 2017 it is projected that 44 percent of Vancouver's population will be immigrants?

VISIBLE MINORITIES (2006, VANCOUVER CMA)

More than 47 percent of Vancouverites (about 875,300 people) are members of visible minority groups. Of these, 2.5 percent claim membership in multiple visible minority groups. Here is the breakdown of those who claim membership in one visible minority group:

Chinese   46.6 percent
South Asian   23.7 percent

The Two Sisters

One of Vancouver's mountain ranges to the north of the city is home to two prominent peaks, 'The Lions of Vancouver.' Native legend describes their origins, which have been known as 'The Two Sisters' or 'The Chief's Daughters.'

Tradition has it that thousands of years ago, long after the first creation, the Sagalie Tyee—the Great Spirit—had two daughters for whom He was preparing a celebration upon their entrance into womanhood. He planned to have all of His children and creations come together for many days of feasting to celebrate the two daughters who would one day give birth to and raise man-warriors as great as their Great Tyee.

The only snag in the plan was ongoing war with northern tribes who sailed the coast singing war songs. The Great Tyee, however, was not alarmed. Laughing, He remembered His many previous victories over the northern tribes. He determined that after the celebration for His daughters, He would resume His offenses against these enemies.

But before the celebration could begin, the two maidens asked a favour of their Father. Vowing not to deny His special daughters anything, The Great Tyree was shocked at their request; they wanted to broker peace by inviting the warring northern tribes to the celebration.

Thus invited, the long time enemies traveled down the coast, bringing women, children and gifts. The former foes celebrated together and were at peace. So pleased with His daughters for creating this new peace, the Great Tyree made them immortal by placing them high in the mountain ranges, two peaks above the rest, for eternity.

Filipino	9.0 percent
Korean	5.1 percent
Southeast Asian	3.8 percent
West Asian	3.2 percent
Japanese	2.9 percent
Latin American	2.6 percent
Black	2.4 percent
Arab	0.8 percent

Source: Statistics Canada.

Laws of Exclusion

When the CPR was complete, Chinese railway labourers who were banned in 1882 from entering the United States sought to make their lives and settle their families (who were still in China) in Vancouver. The Canadian government had other ideas.

The last CPR spike was barely driven when Ottawa introduced a head tax of $50 for each Chinese person wanting to immigrate to Canada. It would be increased to $100 and then $500 in 1902 and 1903, seriously undermining Chinese immigration to Canada.

With the demise of the gold rush by about 1907, Vancouver's economy was in ruins and the Chinese and Japanese became scapegoats. Anti-Asian sentiment reached the breaking point in September of that year, when 9,000 members of the Asiatic Exclusion League swarmed through Chinatown and Japantown, smashing windows, signs and other property.

Anti-Asian feelings remained high and in 1923 the Federal government passed the Chinese Immigration Act, better known as the Exclusion Act, which effectively slammed entirely the door to Chinese immigration. This law remained on the books until 1947.

VANCOUVER IMMIGRANTS (PERCENTAGE OF TOTAL CMA POPULATION)

1986	29 percent
1991	30 percent
1996	35 percent
2001	38 percent
2006	40 percent

Source: Statistics Canada.

MOTHER TONGUE

	Vancouver (CMA)	**British Columbia**
English	56.7 percent	70.6 percent
French	1.2 percent	1.3 percent
French and English	0.1 percent	0.1 percent
Other	42 percent	27.9 percent

They Said It

"Go out...and try to understand what these people want and what they are after."

– Chief Maquinna, seeing Cook's ship in Nootka Sound on March 30, 1778.

SHARING INFORMATION

The City of Vancouver offers several services in the dominant mother tongues of its residents. In addition to publishing its *Guide to Municipal Services* in English, Chinese and Vietnamese, the city also offers welcome literature and phonelines that provide basic city information in Chinese, Punjabi, Spanish and Vietnamese.

All Vancouver Public Libraries also offer multilingual services and hold collections in Chinese, French, German, Japanese, Hindi, Italian, Korean, Portuguese, Punjabi, Russian, Spanish, Tagalog, Polish and Vietnamese. In addition, the Central Library offers a Language Lab and six library branches have Learning Centres that offer assistance in learning English.

Source: City of Vancouver.

MEDIAN FAMILY INCOME IN VANCOUVER

Family Type	Median Family Income	
	2000	2005
Non-immigrant	$78,203	$80,127
Immigrant	$60,316	$59,761

Source: Statistics Canada.

DATE OF ARRIVAL

Of the nearly 40 percent of Vancouverites who are immigrants, approximately 47 percent came to the city before 1991, 35 percent arrived between 1991 and 2000, and 18 percent took up residence here between 2001 and 2006.

Source: Statistics Canada.

FIRST NATIONS

More than 10,000 years before the Spanish sailed the British Columbia coast, the Pacific Northwest was home to many, including the Coast Salish people. Three groups of Coast Salish, the Squamish, the Musqueam and the Tsleil-Waututh, lived and still live, in what today is Metro Vancouver.

These groups spoke each others' languages, intermarried and worked, traded and celebrated together, surviving off the flora and fauna of their land and sea. Forests provided game and cedar trees for building and woodworking, the mountains were home to cougars and mountain goats and the sea yielded orcas and salmon.

COAST SALISH ART

Coast Salish art is distinguished by bold form-lines that flow throughout the artwork consistently and deliberately, outlining figures and creating design. Geometric shapes, dots and dashes are fashioned into human and animal forms. These lines and shapes and their powerful bold colours make Coastal indigenous art recognizable and valued worldwide.

Source: Canadian Encyclopedia.

They Said It

"Without the great effort of Chinese labourers, the CPR could not have been finished on schedule, and the resources of western Canada could not also be explored."

– Sir John A. Macdonald, Prime Minister, 1884.

GIVE-AWAY CEREMONY

The Potlatch was an important celebration among Pacific Coast First Nations, particularly the Coast Salish. Held to mark important milestones such as births, deaths, marriages or initiations, potlatches featured lavish feasting that could last for days. But this was not their sole purpose — they also reinforced social status.

Hosts bestowed upon guests valuable gifts and in so doing affirmed their own social status. The more powerful the host, the more grandiose was the gift-giving. Gifts typically included items such as canoes, food, household goods, slaves and other valuables.

The arrival of Europeans challenged the so-called gift giving ceremony. Missionaries and government officials saw the practice as an impediment to assimilation, banning it in 1884 and making it punishable by fine or imprisonment. Although the Coast Salish ignored the edict outright or found loopholes in the potlatch ban, the prohibition took a toll on this important cultural practice and remained in place until 1951.

Sources: Museum of Anthropology; Canadian Encyclopedia; Harvard College.

They Said It

"Chinamen of the Province of British Columbia may not make application to have their names inserted in any list of voters and are disqualified from voting at any elections."

– Government of British Columbia, 1874.

> "Chinese seethe over Freeway."
> – A *Vancouver Sun* headline announcing Chinese
> opposition to plans to run a highway through Chinatown

CARVINGS

Aboriginals of the Pacific North West are world renowned for their woodworking. While the southern Coast Salish have long carved lavish wooden canoes and house poles, those in the north developed sophisticated totem poles.

Totems and house poles represent families and their histories. Images of beavers, bears, wolves, sharks and birds convey different elements of family history and lineage, helping groups identify each other. Frequently erected at potlatches, totems and house poles often asserted the dominance of a certain clan.

Though totems were likely fixtures for First Peoples in a pre-European landscape, the arrival of metal woodworking tools with Europeans made easier their construction. The most well known totems in existence today were carved and erected after the mid-nineteenth century.

Source: Canadian Encyclopedia.

> "The mountain is also our back up, [our] support and that support is the [supply] of immigrants. We need the new people, we need the new people to keep the city exciting. Of course you can also say they create the traffic problem and a lot of immigrants create unemployment, but no matter, from the overall aspect . . . we can bring the people, we can bring the money, we can bring the business." "
> – Sherman Tai, an immigrant to Richmond from Hong Kong, in an interview on Vancouver's immigration trends, in the *Globe and Mail*, 2006.

Vancouver's Chinatown(s)

Chinese who settled in Vancouver in the late 19th century found work primarily in the 1st Street area. Over time, more and more Chinese looking for social networks and the comfort of numbers in a hostile town settled in the area. 'Shanghai Alley,' as Chinatown was first known, was an isolated neighbourhood, with Chinese businesses and customers supporting each other with little influence from the non-Chinese populations of the rest of the city.

This isolation, a sign of the power of racism, was also a source of community strength, allowing its residents the chance to build and maintain a distinct way of life and culture that still exists today. The isolation that once characterized Chinatown is no more. Today the community is a hub of economic and cultural activity that serves all Vancouverites and it has grown into Canada's largest Chinatown and the third largest in North America, after New York and San Francisco.

Chinese-Vancouverites are a cultural and political force in the city. Since the 1990s, Chinese newcomers to Vancouver have settled outside Chinatown, many in suburbs of the Lower Mainland, particularly around 41st Avenue and Victoria Street in Vancouver. In Richmond, an area called the Golden Village is renowned for its Asian-themed shopping malls and is now home to Canada's second largest Chinese community — many of them immigrants from Hong Kong. In addition to Richmond, Chinese immigrant communities are developing in Burnaby and Coquitlam.

Still, Chinatown remains the vibrant heart of Chinese Vancouver. In recent years, the City of Vancouver's Chinatown Revitalization Program has been working to simultaneously preserve the heritage of, and bring new life to, Chinatown.

TODAY'S FIRST NATIONS SCENE

Vancouver has a population of approximately 2.1 million people. Of these, 40,310, or nearly two percent, identify themselves as Aboriginal.

- North American Indians: 23,515
- Métis: 15,070
- Inuit: 210
- Multiple responses: 525
- None of these categories: 990

RESERVATIONS

In 2006, 7,550 Native people lived on 17 Greater Vancouver area reservations, up 11.7 percent over 2005. In total, these reserves cover 15.2 km². The most populous reserve is Capilano with 2,492 residents.

Source: BC Statistics.

IMPRINT OF EMPIRE

After a brief contest with Spain, British colonists made Vancouver in their image and, as in most of Canada, people with roots in the British Isles have dominated Vancouver's population. As a British colony and then as a Canadian province, the powers-that-be took great pains to make British Columbia a "British" place and fear of American annexation was very real until British Columbia's Confederation in 1871.

As Vancouver expanded, construction of buildings and homes and the designs of gardens and other public spaces reinforced ties to Britain, which remain evident today in place names such as English Bay and the famous park named after British Lord Stanley.

Sources: Statistics Canada; Discover Vancouver; Vancouver.com.

Did you know...

that in 1971 the provincial government designated Chinatown a national historic site?

They Said It

"If it weren't for the Italian immigrants [with their commercial interests] Vancouver's Grandview area would be dead, a slum area which would degenerate those living in and around it." "

– From *The Province*, February 25, 1965.

ASIAN INFLUENCE

People of Asian descent have been part of Vancouver's fabric since its founding. The Chinese were the first to arrive in the middle of the 19th century, enticed by gold and employment opportunities in the fishery and coalmines. Later on, 10,000 Chinese were contracted to build Canadian Pacific Railway (CPR).

Racism and exclusionary laws, such as a sizeable head tax, didn't stop Asian immigration and through the Second World War many Chinese crossed the Pacific to join their families and friends in the city. Here they became members of well-established communities — complete with Chinese language schools, churches, newspapers and radio stations.

The last three decades of the 20th century saw a renewed influx of Asian immigration to Vancouver. The 1975 end of the Vietnam War was accompanied by a crackdown by the Communist North Vietnamese government, a situation that compelled a mass exodus from that nation. Then, in the 1980s and 1990s, as the July 1997 date for the Hong Kong changeover from British to Chinese rule drew near, Hongkongers, concerned what the change would mean for them, also chose to come to Canada, many to Vancouver. Between 1981 and 2001, as numbers of immigrants from North America, Western Europe and Oceania declined, those from West, South and East Asia increased markedly.

They Said It

STRATHCONA PROTEST

For decades, Chinese immigrants to Vancouver were denied basic rights as citizens. It wasn't until 1947 that they were granted the right to vote.

Vancouver's Chinese residents did not sit back, however, and allow the city to run a freeway through their community. In the 1950s, the city proposed the construction of a waterfront highway — and they recommended tearing down 600 homes in Strathcona, in the heart of Chinatown, to do it.

Chinatown residents were joined by other outraged citizens. At first the protest was ignored (the city determined that Chinatown was a slum area that warranted dismantlement). When the protest showed no signs of going away, city officials had no choice but to scuttle it. The protest represented a tuning point in civic affairs in the city.

Source: City of Vancouver; Reflections of Vancouver Historic Chinatown.

GOOD MORNING

The Vancouver Film Office suggests filmmakers working in Chinatown learn the following:

Good Morning: "Jo Sun"
I'm sorry / Excuse me: "Duh Em Ju"
Filming in progress: "Pak Gun Hey"

Did you know...

that the *Chinese Times* newspaper has been published in Vancouver's Chinatown since 1914?

GUNG HAY FAT CHOY!

Vancouver's Chinese New Year celebrations go on for two weeks around the Lunar New Year, which, in the Gregorian calendar can fall anytime between January 21 and February 20. Not only is it one of the biggest festivals in Vancouver, it's one of the largest Chinese New Year celebrations in North America.

Each year more than 50,000 spectators line the parade route along Pender, Gore and Keefer Streets in the heart of Chinatown. In 2008, celebrants rang in the Year of the Rat on February 10; 2009 will see the city ring in the Year of the Ox on February 1 and the year of the Tiger on February 14 in 2010.

The parade has more than 50 traditional lion dance troupes, the largest assembly of traditional lion dancers in Canada. The dancers weave through the streets ornately costumed in playfully fearsome dragon bodies. Dancers are accompanied by burning incense, fire-crackers and drumming.

Sources: Chinatown Vancouver; University of British Columbia, Chinese Benevolent Association of Vancouver.

JAPANTOWN

Vancouver's lumber mills and fish canneries first attracted Japanese immigrants in the 1890s. Like their Chinese counterparts, Japanese newcomers were often viewed as a threat by their European counter-parts. Many Japanese chose to settle en mass in Little Tokyo or Japantown, an area on Powell Street between Gore and Dunlevy.

In 1906, the Vancouver Buddhist Church was built to serve the community. In 1907, the town was ravaged by an attack of the Asiatic Exclusion League, whose stated intent was to rid the city of Asians.

Did you know...

that the company that makes Olivieri pasta and sauces (staples in Canadian grocery stores) was born in Vancouver's little Italy three decades ago?

During World War II, many residents were interned and the community's church was seized by federal government and would not be returned until after the war.

Today Japantown is home to Japanese schools and Japanese-run shops and restaurants, which are known for sushi prepared with fresh Pacific salmon. Each summer the Powell Street Festival celebrates Vancouver's Japanese heritage.

Meanwhile a "New Japantown" is emerging in Vancouver. Also known as Little Ginza, and located on Alberni Street between the West End and Downtown Vancouver, the area has become home to upscale restaurants, boutiques, karaoke bars and dance clubs.

Sources: Virtual Vancouver; Vancouver Buddist Church; Powell Street Festival; Vancouver Buddhist Church.

GERMANS

Germans were part of the first major influx of immigrants to BC in 1857. Part of an urban middle class of shopkeepers, artisans and merchants, they became central to the early social and political life of a young Vancouver. In the early 20th century, more Germans arrived.

WWI was difficult for German Canadian families in Vancouver. They were vilified along with their homeland, their newspapers and churches. When war waged again in 1939, Germans, like other "enemy aliens," such as the Japanese, were interned (the restrictions for Germans were lessened in 1941).

Between 1947 and 1967, more than 300,000 Germans landed in BC, where, unlike Greeks, Italians and different groups of Asian immigrants who established their own enclaves, they melded into the mainstream. Post-war German immigrants to Vancouver settled along Fraser Street and on Robson Street where they opened successful businesses and restaurants. Today 203,715 Vancouverites claim some German heritage.

LITTLE ITALY

There were two distinct waves of Italian immigration to the city, one preceding the First World War, and one directly after the Second

World War. Many came to work the railway and others to set up shops and work in construction. Little Italy was a well established community by the 1930s. This Italian community today stretches from 1st to 12th avenues and is home to more than 30,000 Italian-Canadians and a literal feast of Italian restaurants, coffee bars and shops.

The Italian community has contributed greatly to the city. The famous Lion statues that guard the Lions Gate Bridge are courtesy of Italian sculptor Charles Marega. Bruno Gerussi, the late star of the Canadian classic television series, *The Beachcombers*, is a product of the Vancouver Italian community.

GREEKTOWN

In the 1960s and 70s, many Greek people fled the iron-fisted dictatorship of Georgios Papadopoulos and found a new home in Kitsilano. What emerged was "Greektown," centred at West Broadway on Macdonald Street, and anchored by St. George's Greek Orthodox Church.

In the 1980s, the Greek Community waned somewhat as the result of rising property costs. Greek language newspapers and a television station closed as Greeks moved to different parts of the city. A Greek Day, celebrated by the city since 1974, was cancelled in 1988.

Despite this downturn, Greektown retains a place in Vancouver's cultural map. Each October, St. George's Hellenic Community (which is affiliated with the church) celebrates a Greek Food Festival and in 2005 a citywide Greek Day was reestablished and has been held every year since.

BOAT PEOPLE

In the 1970s, they were simply known as "Boat People." In truth they were the thousands of Vietnamese refugees who risked their lives on leaky ships in pirate-riddled waters to flee their southeast Asian homeland and a ruthless Communist government.

In 1978, the *Hai Hong*, a freighter packed with 2,500 Vietnamese refugees, anchored off Malaysia and issued public pleas for rescue. Canadians responded and in November the first fifteen of 150 Vietnamese refugees arrived in Vancouver.

In 1979, the BC government passed special legislation aimed at helping southeast Asian immigrants settle in the province. A year later, the City of Vancouver created a special Task Force on the Boat People Rescue Project and opened a refugee-coordinating centre where Vancouverites learned how to sponsor, or in other ways aid, the refugees.

Between 1975 and 1985, approximately 111,000 southeast Asian "Boat People" came to Canada, 14,000 of them to BC. Before long, those who came to Vancouver were making their mark of the city as they opened stores and restaurants, particularly in Vancouver's east end and in Surrey.

KOREAN ENCLAVES

A relaxed trade agreement between Canada and Korea in 1994 and a booming Korean economy has meant that Koreans have been coming to Vancouver in record numbers since the 1990s. In fact, approximately 46,000 people of Korean descent now call Greater Vancouver home. Together they have established more than 40 Korean churches, three Korean-language newspapers and a community centre.

The main Korean community in Vancouver is located downtown, on Robson Street in the city's north end. This area is home to an H-Mart, a large restaurant and grocery store offering Korean fare. To buy Korean products, Vancouverites can also go to North Road, on the boundary of Burnaby and Coquitlam, Kingsway in Vancouver or Surrey's Guildford Mall.

Source: Discover Vancouver; Statistics Canada.

PUNJABI MARKET

Approximately 181,895 Indo-Canadians live in Vancouver, more than in any other Canadian city, with the exception of Toronto. The economic and cultural lives of Vancouver Indians are centred at the

Punjabi Market, also called "Little India." Stretching five blocks along Main Street from East 48th to 51st Street avenues, the Punjabi Market offers the food, fashions and entertainment (Bollywood movies).

Each April, the Vancouver Indian community celebrates Vaisakhi. Crowds of 200,000 enjoy a massive parade and Sikh faithful come together to celebrate the birth of their religion.

In 2008, plans are afoot to mark the entrance to this amazing neighborhood with a so-called "Indian Gate"—an Indian-stylized gated entrance much like the Millennium Gate that welcomes visitors to Chinatown.

Sources: CBC; Home & Abroad; Statistics Canada.

Weblinks

Vancouver Multicultural Society

www.urbancultures.ca/welcome.htm
Find out the multicultural happenings in Vancouver at the website of the Vancouver Multicultural Society. Established in 1974, it is the oldest non-profit organization in BC.

First Nations Summit

www.fns.bc.ca
This online home of the First Nations Summit offers much information on the First Nations of British Columbia and the issues that affect them as a community.

Royal BC Museum

www.bcarchives.gov.bc.ca/index.htm
The Royal BC Museum's BC Archives is where the history of the province's First Nations and those from all other nations that make up the province, can be studied.

Culture

The cultural landscape of Vancouver has been shaped by geography and history, operating on the far western fringes of the continent. As a result it has developed its own distinct vibe. It is part of the Canadian mosaic but looks as much to Seattle, San Francisco and Los Angeles as it does to any points eastward. The city has been enriched and informed by its immigrant class and by the small town folks from across the prairies and around BC who have made their way here.

From the vibrant jazz underworld of the roaring 20s and 30s through to the influential punk and indie scenes of the last thirty years, Vancouver musicians have eschewed convention. The Vancouver art world has developed its own distinctive "Vancouver School."

The city has also emerged as one of Canada's foremost centres for more formal cultural offerings. The Vancouver Symphony Orchestra and Ballet British Columbia are recognized around North America. City art galleries, notably the flagship Vancouver Art Gallery, are among the best in the country and are perennially hot tickets in a city with more artists per capita than any other in the country.

Vancouver multicultural influences have come to bear in its literature, cuisine, music, dance and art. In Vancouver, it is possible to marvel at the bold strokes and exquisite carvings in Aboriginal art galleries, see the colour and flavour of the Dragon and Lion dances of Chinese festivals, and enjoy authentic East Indian cuisine, perhaps better than anything you might find in New Deli.

Film is not just wishful thinking here, it is a bona fide industry. The familiar backdrop of Vancouver streets and landscapes may not be familiar to all North Americans, but they are to those of us who live here.

ARTISTS

- Number of artists in Vancouver: 7,250 (Number of artists in Canada: 130,700)
- 21 percent are producers, directors, choreographers and/or in related fields
- 17 percent are actors
- 17 percent are musicians and/or singers
- 16 percent are writers
- 10 percent are artisans and/or craftspeople
- 11 percent are painters, sculptors and/or other visual artists
- 4 percent are dancers
- 3 percent are other performers
- 2 percent are conductors, composers and/or arrangers

They Said It

"I think a new kind of art has emerged since the '70s, a kind that is easier to appreciate, more like entertainment, more attached to media attitudes. The new contemporary art has by now become the dominant form. It's much closer to entertainment and depends on production value and on spectacle in a way that serious art never did before."

– Vancouver photographer Jeff Wall of the
so-called "Vancouver School."

Vancouver X-file

Although Douglas Coupland was born on a Canadian Air Force base in Germany, he grew up in Vancouver and graduated in 1979 from Sentinel Secondary School in West Vancouver. After a failed stint of physics study at McGill in Montreal, Coupland returned to Vancouver to study sculpture at the Emily Carr College of Art & Design.

The study of art and design has had a profound influence on Coupland's life and writing. You see it not only in choice of subject material but in the visual presentation of books like *Terry* (about Canadian icon Terry Fox) or *City of Glass*, his wonderfully eclectic and controversial homage to Vancouver.

After graduating from Emily Carr, Coupland continued his study of art and industrial design in Hawaii, the European Design Institute in Milan and the Hokkaido College of Art and Design in Sapporo, Japan. Strangely it was in Japan studying art that Coupland's writing career could be said to have begun in earnest.

A local Vancouver editor saw a postcard Coupland had written and hired him to write a story on a Los Angeles art dealer. In 1986, he started writing for Vancouver area magazines with a particular interest in pop culture. In 1988, he moved to Toronto to work for a magazine called *Vista*. Although that magazine would go under, a New York publisher came calling and asked the young Coupland if he would write a guide to his generation (the company published the *Yuppie Handbook* and was looking for a similar title for the next generation).

The book, of course, became *Generation X: Tales for an Accelerated Culture*, and launched Coupland as an international superstar. To his credit, Coupland has resisted the pull of fame. When the world press was looking to presage the young Coupland into a tidy category, he said, "I speak for myself, not for a generation."

Although Coupland is never going to be anybody's homeboy, he is nonetheless a devoted Vancouverite and Canadian. He is interested in and by the world around him and by geographical extension that luckily that has meant Vancouver and icons like Terry Fox.

ALL IN A YEAR'S WORK

- Writers: $37,571
- Producers, Directors, and Choreographers: $46,179
- Actors: $24,983
- Artisans and Craftspersons: $21,554
- Painters and Sculptors: $16,800
- Dancers: $19,174
- Musicians and Singers: $19,619

Source: Canada Council.

Hollywood North

Unlike other Canadian jurisdictions, the film business really is a bona fide industry here. In Vancouver, movie and television sets are common enough occurrences that they are mentioned in traffic reports. Virtually everyone in the city knows someone who has worked, or is working, in the film business.

In the last twenty years the film industry in has taken off, encouraged by tax incentives, business support, and a talented film production workforce. In 1978, the BC film industry was worth $12 million but by 2007 that figure had jumped to more than $943 million.

The province is the third largest production centre in North America — only New York and Los Angeles make more films and television shows. The year 2007 was not, however, the industry's best year. That year, 138 Canadian productions and 64 foreign productions were made in the province, down from 144 Canadian and 86 foreign productions in 2006. This decline, though, is at least partly attributable to a writers' strike that crippled the entire North American film industry in 2007 and a high Canadian dollar.

Canadian productions in 2007 included 24 features/DVD features (such as *The Cycle* and *Thirst*), 24 television series (*About a Girl* and *JPod*) , 80 television movies, miniseries, pilots or docu-

THAT'S AN ORDER

A total of 270 citizens of the City of Vancouver have been given the Order of Canada:

- 152 Members
- 99 Officers
- 19 Companions

Source: Governor General of Canada

mentaries (*Pure Evil and Death in the Forest*) and 10 animations (*Storm Hawks* and *Class of the Titans 2*). Its domestic productions included 23 features (*Juno* and *The Watchman*), 18 television series (*Battlestar Galactica*, *Eureka* and *Smallville*), 14 television movies, miniseries, pilots or documentaries (*Bionic Woman* and *Snow Demon*), and 9 animations (*Space Chimps* and *Barbie: Island Princess*).

Vancouver is home to two of the country's largest studios, Lion's Gate Studios and Vancouver Film Studio. The industry now includes hundreds of smaller film and video companies, talent agencies, post-production facilities, and shooting stages. In 2007, an estimated 36,000 people found direct and indirect fulltime employment in the film industry that earned for the province nearly $1.2 billion in spending.

TOTAL DOMESTIC AND FOREIGN BC FILM PRODUCTIONS, 2003-2007

Year	Productions
2003	169
2004	194
2005	211
2006	230
2007	202

VAN-LIT

Vancouver may not have as long and storied a literary history as Montreal or Toronto, but it does have its own stable of iconic writers, as well as a group of up-and-comers who are attempting to establish Vancouver as Canada's literary hotbed.

Douglas Coupland is probably Vancouver's best-known writer internationally; in 2007 he published *The Gum Thief*, his eleventh novel dating back to his 1991 breakthrough, *Generation X: Tales for an Accelerated Culture*. He also wrote a non-fiction ode to the city called *City of Glass* (2000).

The city's other best-known writer is American-born sci-fi visionary William Gibson, who has lived here since 1972. His seminal 1984 novel, *Neuromancer*, shaped the cyberpunk genre, and he has written six more novels, including *Spook Country* (2007), which is partially set in the city.

Vancouver's Asian community is well represented in literary terms. Joy Kogawa's *Obasan* (1981) is the definitive description of the terrible treatment of Japanese Canadians during World War Two. Although Wayson Choy has lived in Toronto since the 1960s, his novels, *The Jade Peony* (1995) and *All That Matters* (2004), are based on his childhood growing up in Vancouver's Chinatown. More recently, Jen Sookfong Lee wrote *The End of East*, in which the city is described in multiple time periods.

The biggest Vancouver book of the past decade was Timothy Taylor's *Stanley Park* (2001). He followed it with another very Vancouver novel, *Story House*, in 2006. There are several graduates of UBC's prestigious Creative Writing program who have written books set here, too, including Nancy Lee (*Dead Girls*), Madeleine Thien (*Simple Recipes* and *Certainty*) and Annabel Lyon (*Oxygen* and *The Best Thing for Me*).

They Said It

"Vancouver is very clean and very lovely. You have to use Canadian money, though. It's very strange."
– **Charlize Theron, talking about filming Reindeer Games on location.**

HAL WAKE'S FIVE MOST INFLUENTIAL BC WRITERS

Hal Wake has been engaged with the literary community in Canada for more than 30 years. In the mid '80s, he was the book producer for CBC Radio's Morningside with Peter Gzowski. He is currently the Artistic Director of the Vancouver International Writers Festival and has hosted literary events at Festivals in Vancouver, Victoria, Whitehorse, New York, London and Sydney Australia.

1. **Pauline Johnson** (1861-1913) was a Mohawk poet, writer and performer. She was the first woman (other than the Queen), the first writer, and the first aboriginal Canadian to be honoured with a commemorative Canadian stamp. Margaret Atwood has been commissioned to write the libretto of a chamber opera about her.

2. **Ethel Wilson** (1888-1980) didn't publish her first novel until she was almost 60, but her second novel, *Swamp Angel*, has become a Canadian classic. She was one of the first Canadian writers to capture the rugged and remarkable beauty of the British Columbia landscape. The award for the best book of fiction by a BC author, awarded annually as one of the BC Book Prizes is named in her honour.

3. **Earle Birney** (1904-1995) was a novelist, playwright and one of the greatest Canadian poets of the 20th century. He won the Governor General's award twice and his poem, "David," has been taught in Canadian schools for more than 50 years. He also founded Canada's first creative writing school at the University of British Columbia.

4. **Douglas Coupland** is an artist and author of fiction and non-fiction whose work has been translated into 35 languages and published in 30 countries. Satirical, insightful and inventive, Coupland's work describes and deconstructs life in contemporary North America. He is one writer the rest of the world turns to in order to probe our cultural calamities.

5. **William Gibson** is one of the most highly acclaimed North American science fiction writers. His novel *Neuromancer* was the first to win the Nebula, Hugo and Phillip K. Dick awards for science fiction. He is the foremost chronicler of our modern technological world and his visions of where technology may take us have often turned out to be uncannily accurate. He is the originator of the term "cyberspace."

CULTURAL SPENDING

Vancouverites spend about $1.7 billion, about $810 per person, on cultural events each year, putting them in seventh place in the country behind Ottawa-Hull, Victoria, Calgary, Edmonton, Regina and Halifax. Cultural spending accounts for 3.3 percent of all consumer spending in Vancouver and 54 percent of cultural spending in all of British Columbia.

- 51 percent to home entertainment
- 21 percent to reading material
- 11 percent to art works and events
- 9 percent to photographic equipment and services
- 6 percent to movie admissions
- 4 percent to art supplies and musical instruments

Source: Hill Strategies Research Inc.

Did you know...

that 51 percent of people living in Vancouver have a library card and they borrow almost 10 million different materials a year? The reference desk also answered 988,713 questions last year.

Take 5 GARY BARCLAY'S FIVE UP AND
COMING VANCOUVER MUSICIANS TO WATCH

Gary Barclay is a freelance music broadcaster and writer who contributes to a variety of media including CBC radio and National Public Radio. Gary hosted the All-Night Jazz Show on CHQM and QM/FM in Vancouver for 14 years. He has conducted hundreds of interviews — primarily in hotel rooms and backstage dressing rooms — with many jazz and blues musicians who have passed through town. Barclay is now transforming his collection of tapes into a sound archive of jazz oral history, with the working title "Jazz Verbatim." Barclay is currently the Associate Editor, Arts & Entertainment, for *Vancouver's Lifestyle Magazine*. These are Gary's top five picks for upcoming Vancouver musicians to watch.

1. **Amanda Tosoff**, a 24-year-old jazz pianist whose quartet, the Amanda Tosoff Quartet, won a CBC Galaxie Rising Star Award in 2007. She's going places.

2. **Jodi Proznick**, a jazz bass player who was awarded Bassist of the Year at the 2008 National Jazz Awards. Her group, the Jodi Proznick Quartet, was awarded the Acoustic Group of the year and their album Foundations was given the Album of the Year honour.

3. **Hayley Sales**, a 21-year-old singer-songwriter in the folk/rock genre. Hayley has recently toured the United Kingdom and Scandinavia and her album has been released in Australia, Japan, Europe and of course Canada. She already gets airplay in Vancouver and performed at the 2008 Vancouver Folk Music Festival.

4. **Chris Ghidoni**, a Manitoba-born, strat-wielding blues guitarist who has earned a reputation as a fierce player with lots of musical attitude since moving to Vancouver. She has given memorable performances at The Yale and The Backstage Lounge, displaying a wide range of style.

5. **Celso Machado**, now a Vancouver resident, this world music specialist from Brazil has been nominated four times for the Juno Best World Music Album.

City as Star

Vancouver is very clearly Chris Haddock's town, and strangely enough they've both made stars out of each other. Haddock's Vancouver is thankfully very different than the standard bumpf that fills the pages of the tourist literature. Haddock's Vancouver is Gassy Jack's Vancouver, the underworld, the unacknowledged neighbourhoods such as the Downtown Eastside. And those neighbourhoods are populated by people . . . real people. Hustlers, drug dealers, smugglers and police and you are never certain who the good or bad guys are.

Although Haddock was born into a comfortable middle class Kitsilano family (his father taught forestry at UBC), Haddock chose to be on the outside looking in. He busked for years playing violin outside the liquor store on Broadway and Maple, often taking day labourer work to make ends meet. In the 1990s he graduated to the Vancouver club scene, playing not violin but bass guitar with the group the Questionnaires.

In the mid 80s, Haddock got a gig to help write the theme song for an American television show, which in turn led to him writing scripts for Vancouver-shot shows *MacGyver* and *Airwolf*. Hollywood beckoned and before he knew it, Haddock was in Los Angeles writing (and rewriting) scripts. It paid well but like the gristle on a well cooked steak, you eat enough of it and it can kill you.

It was killing Haddock and in 1995 he was back in Vancouver for good. He had balls in the air, though, and one of those balls was a pitch for a gritty new series called *DaVinci's Inquest* that featured the city and the province's chief coroner as its story line. It ran for seven years, winning more than 50 Junos. The country's best television was now being made in Vancouver and not Toronto.

The cancellation of Haddock's new series *Intelligence* in the summer of 2008 seems like a CBC misstep. It had all of the Haddock trademarks: it was smart, full of surprise and intrigue, and again made the city of Vancouver a star. Tourist literature has made much of the mountains, ocean and the weather. Haddock has not so quietly filled in the blanks and he is likely to do so for a long time to come.

They Said It

"I don't feel that this is unfair. That's the thing about cancer. I'm not the only one, it happens all the time to people. I'm not special. This just intensifies what I did. It gives more meaning. It'll inspire more people. I just wish people would realize that anything's possible if you try; dreams are made possible if you try."

– Terry Fox

RECOGNITION FOR THE ARTS

In 2005-2006, artists and art organizations in British Columbia received $17.4 million from the Canada Council for the Arts, with an additional $1.2 million given to 2,182 authors through the Public Lending Right Program. Of these funds, 72 percent went to artists and organizations in Vancouver. Organizations in the city that received funding included the Vancouver Opera Association, the Vancouver Symphony, the Arts Club Theatre and the Vancouver Art Gallery.

Source: Canada Council.

LITERATURE

Four Vancouver-based writers have been nominated for the Scotiabank Giller Award: Timothy Taylor for *Stanley Park* in 2001, Bill Gaston for *Mount Appetite* in 2002, Pauline Holdstock for *Beyond Measure* in 2004 and Wayson Choy for *All That Matters* in 2004.

Source: Scotiabank Giller Prize webpage.

VANCOUVER BOOK AWARD WINNERS

- 2007 Michael Kluckner, *Vancouver Remembered* (Whitecap Books)
- 2006 Jean Barman, *Stanley Park's Secret: The Forgotten Families of Whoi Whoi, Kanaka Ranch and Brockton Point* (Harbour Publishing) and James Delgado, *Waterfront* (Stanton Atkins & Dosil)
- 2005 Lance Berelowitz, *Dream City: Vancouver and the Global Imagination* (Douglas & McIntyre)
- 2004 Daniel Francis, *L.D.: Mayor Louis Taylor and the Rise of*

Vancouver (Arsenal Pulp Press)

- 2003 Lincoln Clarkes, *Heroines*, essays by *Ken Dietrich et al.* (Anvil Press) and Reid Shier, ed, *Stan Douglas: Every Building on 100 Block West Hastings* (Contemporary Art Gallery/Arsenal Pulp Press)
- 2002 Keith Carlson et al., *A Sto:lo-Coast Salish Historical Atlas* (Douglas and McIntyre)

Source: City of Vancouver.

ALT MUSIC INCUBATOR

Vancouver has long been a hotbed for acts on the musical fringes. From the 1930s to the 1950s, Hogan's Alley, a small black community in Vancouver's east end, was home not just to Blind Pigs, but also to some of the finest jazz and blues musicians. Hogan's Alley attracted the likes of Louis Armstrong and Frank Sinatra, who, after their shows elsewhere in the city, found their way to stages in the small community.

In the 1960s, as the hippie youth movement grew, local bands such as "Mother Tucker's Yellow Duck," "The Collectors" and "Bobby Taylor and the Vancouvers" became the voice of a generation.

By the late 1970s, punk rock bands, such as "DOA," "Subhumans," "The Pointed Sticks" and the "K-Tels," exploded onto the scene, getting their start in Vancouver and finding greater fame in Western Europe and the United States. Throughout the 1980s and 1990s, Vancouver indie bands included "54-40," "No Means No," "Gob," "The Smugglers," "SNFU," the "Black Halos" and "Three Inches of Blood."

More recent indie bands making names for themselves include "Black Mountain," all girl band, "The Organ," and "Pink Mountaintops." The super alt band, the "New Pornographers," and acclaimed front man, Carl Newman, has been named by American Blender magazine as one of the top 100 music visionaries in the world.

FRESH AND LOCAL

In 2005, Vancouver writers and couple Alisa Smith and J.B. MacKinnon decided to go a full year eating only food that had trav-

Bio BILL REID

Bill Reid (1920-1998), one of Canada's greatest artists, was born in Victoria to an American father and Haida First Nations mother. Reid remained largely unaware of Haida culture until his teens and twenties when he spent time with his maternal grandfather who had retained his Haida culture and who himself had worked with the great First Nations artist Charles Edenshaw.

As a young man looking to earn a living Reid landed a job at the CBC in Toronto. During his time there he learned more about Northwest Coast native art by studying Edenshaw's work at the Royal Ontario Museum. Reid also became interested in jewellery making and studied it at Ryerson Institute of Technology.

In 1951, Reid had a chance to return to Vancouver and this is where he became more intensely aware of his Haida heritage and its importance in understanding both himself and the world around him. He studied intently the symbolism of Edenshaw and other First Nations artists.

In 1958, he landed a job with the University of British Columbia to help reconstruct a section of a Haida village. The carvings, through which Reid essentially taught himself the craft of pole-making, were completed in 1962 and are now outdoor exhibits at the UBC Museum of Anthropology.

By 1967, First Nations art was beginning to experience a revival. The work at the carving shed at the Royal B.C. Museum brought the great artist Mungo Martin and Bill Reid into the spotlight and "*Arts of the Raven*" became the first contemporary showing of First Nations art.

Although Vancouver was not the birthplace of Reid or the home to his Haida roots, his presence and artwork has had a tremendous impact on the city's landscape and its artistic reputation. Visitors to the city are greeted by Reid's "Spirit of Haida Gwaii, The Jade Canoe," displayed at the Vancouver International Airport. The "Raven and the First Humans" is displayed at UBC's Museum of Anthropology and "The Chief of the Undersea World" is shown at the Vancouver Aquarium.

Reid was the pivotal force in introducing to the world the great art traditions of the indigenous people of the Northwest Coast of North America. His legacies include infusing that tradition with modern ideas and forms of expression, influencing emerging artists and building lasting bridges between First Nations and other cultures.

When Reid died in1998, his life had come full circle. Friends and relatives paddled a large cedar canoe, carved by Reid for Expo 86, for two days along the Pacific coast to bring his ashes to Tanu Island in Haida Gwaii, the site of his mother's village.

eled less than 100 miles to their kitchen. Their book about this year of eating locally, *The 100-Mile Diet*, has inspired thousands of people to become "locavores." Nowhere is this movement stronger than right here in Vancouver.

Come early to the Saturday morning Trout Lake Farmers Market near Commercial Drive or risk missing out on the heirloom tomatoes, wild mushrooms and a wide range of locally grown organic produce. Offshoot markets in other neighbourhoods, including Kitsilano, the West End and Riley Park, might not be as well known, but are just as busy.

The local food trend is reflected in many of the city's best restaurants with menus highlighting dishes derived from fresh, local ingredients. Raincity Grill offers a comprehensive 100 Mile Tasting Menu, and others such as Aurora Bistro, Bishop's and C all celebrate locally produced food.

For those seeking the opposite of local, a dizzying variety of ethnic cuisine from around the world is also available. Every possible Asian style is represented here, highlighted by Canada's best and freshest sushi. And it's just as easy to find Ethiopian, Ukrainian, Brazilian or Afghani fare.

Did you know...

that although the famed Louis Armstrong and The All Stars recorded a show played at Exhibition Gardens in January 1951, the recording was not released until 2006, more than half a century later?

Did you know...

that *Adbusters* was born in Vancouver in 1989? *Adbusters* is a nonprofit magazine dedicated to the ecology and the exposure of the negative forces of commercialism. It has a circulation of 120,000.

They Said It

"Art can never be understood, but can only be seen as a kind of magic, the most profound and mysterious of all human activities. Within that magic, one of the deepest mysteries is the art of the Northwest Coast, a unique expression of an illiterate people, resembling no other art form except perhaps the most sophisticated calligraphy."

**– Artist Bill Reid in "*Silent Speakers:
The Arts of the Northwest Coast*," by Martine J. Reid.**

CAFÉ CULTURE

When the first Starbucks outlet in Vancouver opened in 1987 many locals smirked and went back to sipping an espresso from one of the many Italian cafés strung along Vancouver's version of Little Italy on Commercial Drive. Many of these same coffee purists later cried foul when the Seattle chain to dared open a branch there, but the fact is it's easy to avoid Starbucks here. Other local chains include Blenz (26 outlets), Bean Around the World (14), Waves (11) and JJ Bean (6). The best of this caffeinated crowd, however, just might be Caffè Artigiano with six outlets in the city and counting.

In the trendy South Main neighbourhood, coffee shops are only outnumbered by the construction cranes crowding the skyline. In one four-block stretch around Main and Broadway there are ten coffee shops, including a mind-boggling three separate Starbucks outlets. And they're all busy, all the time.

Did you know...

that in 2003, Vancouver Mayor Larry Campbell declared December 21st "D.O.A. Day" in honour of the 25th anniversary of the famed Vancouver punk band?

RESTAURANTS

Vancouver's expansive culinary offerings put it on par with any of the world's major cities, but offer much more reasonable prices than their counterparts in Toronto, New York or London. There are more than 4,500 restaurants catering to every pocketbook and taste.

BEER & BREWING

Vancouver is heaven for beer lovers, boasting several brewpubs and craft breweries, including Steamworks, Yaletown Brewing, Dix, R&B, Storm and Granville Island. Add to this mix restaurants that specialize in serving top-notch beers, such as Six Acres and the Alibi Room, which offers 19 BC craft beers on tap. And if that doesn't satisfy your thirst, there are rotating Cask Nights at different restaurants around the city where brewers take turns showing off small-batch experimental brews. But don't be late: the beer only lasts until the firkin runs dry.

THE VAG

In 1931 the Vancouver Art Gallery (VAG) opened its doors on West Georgia Street, offering visitors a small but impressive collection of works by British artist Sir Charles Holmes.

Initially, the VAG focused on British art trends and artists, paying little attention to home grown talent. In the late 1940s, however, there was something of a renaissance in the Vancouver art world as Lawren Harris of the famous Group of Seven helped the gallery develop a new look and feel. By 1983, the gallery was bursting with a growing collection of Canadian and international art and was moved to its current home on Hornby Street, a space renovated by famed Vancouver architect Arthur Erickson.

Today the gallery enjoys one of the largest acquisitions budget in Canada and has a collection of between 7,000 and 9,000 paintings, sculptures, photos, prints and drawings. Perhaps its crowning jewel is the Emily Carr Gallery whose collection is loaned in Canada and internationally.

VANCOUVER SCHOOL

Vancouver has spawned many internationally-renowned visual artists. The most influential of these are known as "The Vancouver School" — a collection of contemporary, photo-based artists including Jeff Wall,

Take 5 MIA STAINSBY'S TOP FIVE
'CHEAP EATS' IN VANCOUVER (UNDER $10)

Mia Stainsby is the restaurant critic and food writer for the *Vancouver Sun*. Restauranteurs would love to know what Ms. Stainsby looks like, but as she says, if they know what she looks like the gig is up. She is one of two critics in the city who does not accept freebies.

1. **Go Fish**, 1504 West First Avenue. A picturesque fish shack overlooking False Creek's Fisherman's Wharf. The food is delicious and the outdoor seating — which is all they have — comes with a picturesque view.

2. **Gallery Cafe and Catering**, 750 Hornby Street. So it's cafeteria-style food, so what! Especially when it's better than most budget places and when the room — particularly the terrace in the summer — is so lovely.

3. **Phnom Penh**, 244 East Georgia Street. This long-time popular spot in Chinatown is home to the best Vietnamese and Cambodian food in town.

4. **Fujiya, 912 Clark Drive**. It's mostly a grocery store but the deli sections are filled with Japanese bento boxes, sushi, side dishes and Japanese pastry. There are even a few tables to sit and eat your purchases.

5. **Kintaro**, 788 Denman Street. Vancouver's own Tampopo. They're dead serious about ramen here and the line-ups into the small noodle joint are a sign of how good it is.

Ian Wallace, Roy Arden, Stan Douglas, Ken Lum and Rodney Graham.

Coined by a French art critic, the term "The Vancouver School" came into use at about the time of Expo '86 when curators and critics started writing about this group of Vancouver artists and their use of complex photographs to comment and reflect on conceptual art, art history and current socio-economic forces. The Vancouver School's photography placed Vancouver in the art world's spotlight.

Sources: Canadian Encyclopedia; Vancouver Art Gallery.

Did you know...

that there are three mascots for the 2010 Olympic Games? They are Minga, a critter that is part bear, part whale, Quatchi, a Sasquatch-type figure and Sumi, an animal spirit whose name comes from the Salish word "Sumesh" meaning "guardian spirit."

TOP FIVE
VANCOUVER FESTIVALS

1. **Celebration of Lights Fireworks Festival**. This festival earns top spot because it attracts 1.5 million people over four nights.
2. **Bard on the Beach Shakespeare Festival**. The city's longest festival runs from May to September each year. It drew 86,000 people in 2006.
3. **Folk Festival**. Loved by locals and visitors alike, this one has been drawing crowds for more than three decades.
4. **Vancouver Pride Parade**. This wildly popular parade kicks off weeklong celebration each August.
5. **Vancouver International Jazz Festival**. Each year it attracts world-class talent.

Source: Tourism Vancouver.

ALL VANCOUVER'S A STAGE

Vancouver's theatre history dates back nearly a century to 1915 when McGill and Harvard grad Frederic Wood joined the faculty of the newly-established University of British Columbia as one of the two original members of the Department of English.

Wood founded the Players' Club, directing all plays staged by students from 1916 to 1931, including semi-annual tours around the province. A campus theatre named after him was built in 1963. He died in 1976, widely credited as having been a major influence in the development of theatre in the city.

They Said It

"This is Vancouver where the culinary bar is raised higher and the restaurants are more trend-setting than anywhere in the United States."

– Tan Vinh, *Seattle Times.*

THE PLAYHOUSE

In terms of professional theatre, Vancouverites had to content themselves with British and American touring productions until 1946 when Everyman Theatre was formed. The inception of the Canada Council for the Arts in 1957 led to the construction of the Queen Elizabeth Theatre here in 1959, which is still the city's primary theatrical venue half a century later.

Its resident company, the Vancouver Playhouse, has been the city's leading theatre company ever since, although in recent years it has been supplanted as Number One in terms of bums in seats by the Arts Club, which operates out of two venues: the Granville Island Stage and the gorgeously restored Stanley Theatre in South Granville.

A BOOM

The 1970s and '80s saw a boom in the number of smaller companies in Vancouver, such as Touchstone Theatre, Théâtre la Seizième and the Firehall Arts Centre.

Bard on the Beach, the city's annual summer Shakespeare festival staged in Vanier Park in open-ended tents with a spectacular backdrop of mountains, sea and sky, has grown from humble origins in 1990 to one of the city's hottest tickets today, attracting more than 85,000 people in 2007. Another important venue is the Vancouver East Cultural Centre, which is celebrating its 35th anniversary with a multi-million-dollar renovation.

ELECTRIC

The latest wave in Vancouver theatre is the exciting growth of innovative "creation companies" such as the Electric Company and Boca del Lupo, devoted to developing and producing their own innovative productions from scratch. Together with the annual PuSH International Performing Arts Festival, these companies are raising the profile of Vancouver theatre on the national stage.

Take 5 TOP FIVE MOST POPULAR ITEMS
ON THE MENU OF WHITE SPOT

Vancouver's own restaurant chain White Spot has serving up tasty eat-in and take-out meals since Nat Bailey opened the franchise's first drive-in on Granville in 1928. In the eight decades since, Vancouverites have come to love the 'Spot', and frequently take in the fun family atmosphere while chomping down some of their favourite local grub.

1. **Triple O's Legendary Platter** - $8.49
2. **Nat Bailey Hearty Breakfast** - $8.99
3. **Pirate Paks** - $5.99
4. **White Spot Fish and Chips** - $9.99
5. **White Spot Clubhouse** - $9.99

THEATRE IN VANCOUVER

- 21 theatre venues
- 2 outdoor theatrical events
- 32 professional groups
- The Fringe International Theatre Festival

Source: Tourism Vancouver.

THE ORPHEUM

Opened in 1927 as one of the West Coast's most extravagant theatres, Vancouver's grand Orpheum Theatre was initially home to a vaudeville stage that welcomed the likes of Charlie Chaplin and the Marx Brothers. Shortly after its burlesque heyday, the venue on Smithe at Seymour served briefly as a movie theatre before becoming one of two homes to the Vancouver Symphony Orchestra (VSO).

In the 1970s, the city purchased and restored the building, reopening it in 1977 as sole home of the VSO. In 1983, the Orpheum got another facelift with the addition of Westcoast Hall, a new foyer that accommodates 3,000 people. Celebrated for its beauty, charm and important place in the city's arts scene, the Orpheum is a designated national historic site.

Take 5 FIVE FAMOUS VANCOUVERITES

1. **Sarah MacLachlan**
2. **Bryan Adams**
3. **Michael Bublé**
4. **Michael J. Fox**
5. **Raymond Burr** (deceased))

Weblinks

Bard on the Beach
www.bardonthebeach.org
Check out the online home of the Bard on the Beach outdoor Shakespeare festival held annually throughout the summer.

Folk Music Festival
www.thefestival.bc.ca
The Vancouver Folk Music Festival has been voted by Vancouverites as the best fest held in the city, see why!

Vancouver Art Gallery
www.vanartgallery.bc.ca
Visit the Vancouver Art Gallery on the web.

Take 5 FIVE FILMS
SHOT IN VANCOUVER

1. **The Butterfly Effect** (2004) starring Ashton Kutcher, Melora Walters
2. **Best in Show** (2000) starring Christopher Guest, Eugene Levy
3. **I, Robot** (2004) Will Smith, Bridget Moynahan
4. **The Accused** (1988) starring Jodie Foster, Kelly McGillis
5. **X-2** (2003) Hugh Jackman, Patrick Stewart

Economy

Natural resources have always been the foundation of Vancouver economic life. First Nations enjoyed a rich lifestyle based on the bounty of the surrounding sea and forest. Early settlers, of course, had to farm, fish and trap to survive. Very early on however, logging and the forestry industry became the backbone of the Vancouver economy.

A sawmill in Moodyville (now the City of North Vancouver) was operating as early as 1863. It was quickly followed by another mill near the foot of what today is Gore Street. For about half a century (1940-1990), forestry was king for the city and province, and it was said that "50 cents of every dollar" came from wood. Today forestry is in a tailspin, with markets drying up and costs skyrocketing.

The choice of Vancouver as the western terminus of the Canadian Pacific Railway made it the transportation hub west of the Rockies. With the completion of the Panama Canal in 1920, Vancouver became one of the most important ports on the West Coast of North America. Resource-rich British Columbia and the western provinces now had a port with which to ship goods to the Pacific Rim.

Over the past twenty years, Vancouver's economy has evolved from one centred on servicing the province's resource economy to one marked by a dynamic urban centre with strong, multi-faceted international connections that have strengthened dramatically with the rise of the economies of Asia Pacific. The Vancouver economy now accounts for more than half of British Columbia's population and economic output.

The economy is now highly diversified thanks to strengths in many new areas including significant clusters in knowledge-based sectors, such as life sciences, digital media, art and entertainment and sustainable industries. The city is also undergoing a construction boom fuelled by the 2010 Olympics.

Newcomers find new reasons to beat a path to Vancouver's door. The red-hot housing market and construction boom reflect the city's popularity as a place to live. Skilled young high-technology workers and retired baby-boomers alike are attracted by its beauty and relaxed lifestyle, not to mention the mild winters. With new and established markets in every direction, particularly with the rise of Asia, Vancouver is no longer Canada's most westerly terminus, but rather at the center of a new economic order.

GDP

Gross Domestic Product represents the total value of goods and services produced.

- Estimated Vancouver total GDP (2007): $64 billion
- Vancouver GDP growth over 2006: 3.1 percent
- Canadian GDP growth over 2006: 2.7 percent
- Vancouver's percentage of the provincial GDP: 53 percent
- Vancouver's percentage of the provincial population: 50 percent

PER CAPITA

- Canadian GDP per capita (2007): $38,200
- BC GDP per capita (2007): $37,258
- Vancouver GDP per capita: $35,887

Did you know...

that the wildly popular children's slippers, Robeez, are made in Vancouver?

Take 5 WANDA BOYD'S TOP FIVE

PROS AND CONS ABOUT RUNNING
A SMALL BUSINESS IN VANCOUVER

Wanda Boyd is the President of K.W. Publishing Ltd., home of *The Prospector Investment* and *Exploration News* and *The Independent Times*.

TOP FIVE PROS

1. The place itself. The Vancouver area is truly beautiful, eye candy for the creative and spiritual soul. The view is a good way to start a hard day's work.

2. Vancouver is a big city, but it's got a small town attitude. People want to do business with their own community and this creates much opportunity for local business.

3. A company marketing a mature audience with one of our publications, we are in a city and province well representing our target market.

4. Vancouver has a tight and loyal business community offering educational and informative support.

5. The atmosphere encourages small business; Vancouver is, after all, a city run by small business.

TOP FIVE CONS

1. It is not Toronto! The long standing friendly rivalry between Toronto and other Canadian cities aside, it is true that if you need to talk to a decision maker you usually need to dial a 416 area code.

2. It is not Toronto! So be prepared to shell out the cost of business travel.

3. The business world on the West Coast is stereotyped as being 'small time.' Perhaps the 2010 Olympics will rectify this.

4. The laid-back attitude for which we are known is not an asset when employers and investors are seeking not-so-laid-back employees and opportunities.

5. Support in western Canada for major services, such as Canada Post, are lacking. Too often issues have to be worked out over the phone to a faceless voice in Ottawa (or Toronto!).

1. **Henrik Sedin**, Captain,Vancouver Canucks: $1,833.30
2. **Bob Elton**, President & CEO of BC Hydro: $241.76
3. **Jim Chu**, Vancouver Police Chief: $112.82
4. **Sam Sullivan**, Mayor of Vancouver: $62.75
5. **City Councillor**, $27.64

Sources: Government of BC; City of Vancouver; BC Hydro; Sportsnet.

BC TAXES

- Small business tax rate: 4.5 percent
- Corporate tax rate: 12 percent

CONSUMPTION TAXES

In Vancouver, two different taxes are applied to products and services. The federal Goods and Services Tax (GST) is 5 percent, while the Provincial Sales Tax (PST) is set at 7.5 percent and applies to the selling price including the GST. Some items including groceries, restaurant meals, and books are PST exempt.

INFLATION

In February 2008, Vancouver's inflation rate stood at 1.3 percent, up from 1.1 percent in 2007. British Columbia's inflation rate stood at 1.1 percent, Canada's at 1.8 percent.

Sources: BC Statistics; Journal of Commerce, "Canada's inflation rate remains subdued in February," March 26, 2008.

Did you know...

that 66 percent of everything that leaves the Port of Vancouver is headed for Asia? Of the rest, 13 percent is shipped to Latin America, 11 percent to Europe and the remainder to various destinations worldwide.

You Said How Much?

Here is what people in various occupations earn on an hourly basis, on average, in and around Metro Vancouver (drawn from the latest available sources):

Dentists	$52.92
Mining engineers	$46.15
Electrical engineers	$41.50
Pharmacists	$39.73
Physiotherapists	$34.99
Registered nurses	$31.83
Medical radiation technologists	$31.42
University professors	$31.19
Secondary school teacher	$30.84
Human resources managers	$29.71
Optometrists	$28.54
Computer programmers and interactive media developers	$27.38
Chiropractors	$25.15
Financial auditors and accountants	$24.29
Authors and writers	$24.24
Carpenters	$21.34
Web designers and developers	$21.26
Community and social service workers	$20.39
Dental Assistant	$20.27
Sheet metal workers	$20.24
Truck drivers	$20.20
Plumbers	$18.52
Automotive service technicians/truck mechanics	$17.02
Bus drivers/transit operators	$16.86
Waterworks and gas maintenance workers	$16.70
Photographers	$15.88
Labourers in mineral and metal processing	$15.65
Chefs	$15.44
Janitors/caretakers/building superintendents	$14.70
Hairstylists and barbers	$11.66
Weavers, knitters and other fabric makers	$10.48
General farm workers	$ 9.67

HOUSEHOLD INCOME (COUPLE FAMILIES)

Median total income from Statistics Canada's latest available data:

- Calgary: $90,700
- Halifax: $75,500
- Toronto: $71,200
- **Vancouver: $68,600**
- Trois Rivieres: $63,000
- Canada: $70,400

Source: Statistics Canada.

COST OF LIVING IN CANADIAN CITIES

(to maintain a standard of living associated with three different income scenarios)

	$60,000	$80,000	$100,000
Edmonton	$61,830	$81,142	$99,902
Calgary	$62,818	$82,109	$105,317
Ottawa	$63,168	$84,102	$104,699
Montreal	$68,167	$92,594	$113,884
Vancouver	**$69,009**	**$90,927**	**$112,647**
Toronto	$74,114	$96,439	$122,627

Source: Edmonton Economic Development Corporation.

Did you know...

that 17,101 Vancouverites worked for the federal government in 2006, representing six percent of all the federal government employees in Canada? Those Vancouver feds earned $80.9 million of the $1.4 billion earned by all federal employees that year.

Bio PATTISON

Little Jimmy Pattison moved to Vancouver from Saskatchewan as an eight-year-old. His father had hit the skids in Saskatoon but found a way out through the church there and moved the family to Vancouver for a fresh start.

Money was tight for all of Pattison's childhood. When the landlord jacked the rent from $25 to $27.50, the Pattisons had to move. In addition to selling cars, his father worked six nights a week in a skid road mission and young Jimmy used to work with him at least three nights a week. The experience for young Jimmy showed just how easily life could go off the rails.

When Pattison decided to follow his father's lead and sell cars, he did very well at it. Better than his old man, and well enough that he got the Royal Bank to back him with a $40,000 loan for a three gas pump, two-car showroom GM franchise that he bought on the corner of 18th and Cambey.

That was fifty years ago, and Pattison could not have imagined from that single franchise he would become chairman of the Jim Pattison Group, the country's third largest privately held company. Today, the company has interests in automotive, media, packaging, food sales and distribution, magazine distribution, entertainment, export and financial industries and in 2007 it had more than $6.4 billion in sales. It has more than 30,000 employees at 410 locations worldwide.

Pattison's personal wealth has been estimated to be close to $1.3 billion. *Forbes* magazine has ranked him among the top 250 richest people in the world. Pattison is a devoted left coaster, taking particular pleasure in tweaking the noses of Bay Street and the Eastern establishment as his fortunes and those of Vancouver and the West Coast continue to rise. In the five years leading up to Vancouver's Expo year he worked almost full time and without compensation to showcase the city. Pattison is a recipient of both the Order of Canada and the Order of British Columbia.

They Said It

WHERE THE MONEY GOES

Here's how Vancouverites spend their money, according to the latest available statistics from Statistics Canada:

	Percentage
Shelter	21.0
Income tax	18.5
Transportation	13.0
Food	11.0
Recreation	5.7
Insurance/pension payments	5.1
Household operation	4.5
Clothing	4.0
Health care	3.2
Education	2.8
Tobacco and alcohol	2.4
Monetary gifts/contributions	2.0
Miscellaneous	1.7
Personal care	1.6
Games of chance	0.5
Reading material	0.4

Source: Statistics Canada.

They Said It

Timber Baron

For more than half a century, Harvey Reginald MacMillan's name was virtually synonymous with forestry in Vancouver. A bushy-eyebrowed Ontarian with a Master's degree in Forestry from Yale, MacMillan (1885-1976) was just 26 when he was hired as BC's first Chief Forester.

He was much too ambitious to settle in for life in a government job. He soon resigned to go into the lumbering business in Chemainuson, Vancouver Island. He quit that job as well with a now legendary vow: "The next time I walk through this door, Mr. Humbird, I am going to own this mill." By 1944, he did.

During a stint with the Imperial Munitions Board during WWI, MacMillan cruised the West Coast looking for Sitka spruce. Old growth spruce had a combination of strength and lightness suitable for making frames for the fighter-planes of the day. After the war, he formed the H.R. MacMillan Export Company to market Douglas fir to overseas markets.

MacMillan saw that owning both the raw material and the means of production was vital to success in the cut-throat, low margin business of lumbering. During the Depression, he began buying sawmills and private timber. Through mergers and acquisitions, MacMillan built one of the most vertically-integrated forest companies in the world. "HR" built an empire that at one time produced 25 percent of the lumber on the BC coast and 38 percent of the market pulp.

From 1917 onward, MacMillan made Vancouver his home and the center for his business operations. He was one of the country's most important and successful entrepreneurs. During his lifetime he was a vital presence in the city. There is the Bloedel Conservatory in Queen Elizabeth Park, the H. R. MacMillan Planetarium, the MacMillan Bloedel Ltd. Canadiana Collection in the public library, and the H. R. MacMillan Gallery of Whales at the Vancouver Aquarium Marine Science Centre, that are some of the better known.

Almost with a whisper, MacMillan's name disappeared from the annals of business in 1999, when Weyerhaeuser Canada absorbed of MacMillan Bloedel Ltd. Brascan Corp (now Brookfield) bought HR's private forestlands in 2005, and they became the basis of Island Timberlands LLC.

> "It's virtually impossible to spend a Pattison-free day in the province."
>
> — **Keith Damsell, in a 1998 article in the *Financial Post*.**

AVERAGE HOUSING MARKET PRICES IN CANADA'S BIGGEST CITIES (2008)

- **Vancouver: $611,613**
- Victoria: $476,639
- Calgary: $418,866
- Toronto: $395,918
- Edmonton: $341,376
- Ottawa: $298,336
- Regina: $242,981
- Halifax: $235,312

Source: Canadian Real Estate Association.

THROUGH THE ROOF

In 2007, housing costs (for a detached two-storey house) in Vancouver became the most unaffordable they have ever been, according to the Royal Bank of Canada (RBC). The RBC says that it would take 72 percent of a $60,000 median salary to afford a lowly detached bungalow.

Did you know...

that more than 3 dozen apparel manufactures (including lululemon) operate out of Vancouver and generate annual sales of more than $100 million? The 2010 Winter Olympic Games promise to offer particular benefits to this industry.

Did you know...

that 54 percent of all BC jobs are located in the greater Vancouver area?

RENTING

In both 2006 and 2007, Metro Vancouver's vacancy rate hovered at 0.7 percent.

	2001	**2007**
Average rent for bachelor apartment	$621	$737
One bedroom	$726	$847
Two bedroom	$919	$1,086
Three bedroom	$1,060	$1,248

Sources: Canadian Mortgage and Housing Corporation.

Next Level

Founded in 2002 by four software industry veterans, Next Level Games Inc. embodies that can-do attitude that has come to typify the Vancouver gaming industry scene. In just over four years, the company has grown from a standing start to more than 110 employees. In 2006, Next Level Games opened a studio in Beijing, China.

The company's first project was *NHL Hitz Pro*, and since then, it also has been working with Nintendo on the *Mario Strikers* series and *Spiderman: Friend or Foe* for publishers that include Sony Corp., Nintendo and Activision Publishing Inc.

The company offers full-service game development and content creation for such platforms as Playstation 3, Xbox 360, and Nintendo Wii. Next Level Games is a licensed developer for Sony, Microsoft and Nintendo, as well as a licensed GameSpy developer.

They Said It

RENTS IN SELECTED METRO AREAS

	1 bedroom	2 bedrooms
Toronto	$901	$1,057
Vancouver	**$847**	**$1,086**
Ottawa	$801	$963
Calgary	$902	$1,116
Edmonton	$784	$958
Montreal	$604	$661
Halifax	$663	$820

Source: Canada Mortgage and Housing Corporation.

NO PARKING

Median cost of monthly parking (unreserved rates)

- Canadian average: $194.51
- Calgary: $350
- Toronto: $300
- Montreal: $259
- Vancouver: $194
- Edmonton: $140

Source: Collier's International.

Did you know...

that entrepreneurs constitute the second largest meetup.com group in Vancouver behind hikers?

Take 5 NORM DUNCAN'S PLACES

TO HAVE A 'SHMOOZING' DOWNTOWN BUSINESS LUNCH

Norm Duncan has lived all of his 52 years in Vancouver. He is married with two children, who are continuing the Duncan tradition of attending UBC. When he's not coaching his son's soccer team or renovating his heritage house — one of the oldest private homes in Metro Vancouver — Norm, a dedicated investment advisor, is schmoozing his way through many a business lunch.

1. **Don Francesco's Restaurant** on Burrard. The best Italian place near the downtown core, this is my favourite schmoozing spot. The food and service are excellent. There are lots of private corners for conversations not for prying ears. Francesco (the owner) is usually there and makes everyone feel welcome.

2. **Hy's Encore** on Hornby. This is a Vancouver tradition — where Vancouver deals and schmoozing have been happening for years. The food is excellent with good service and the room is dark and intimate. You have to try the cheese toast. A great place on dark winter days, too.

3. **Moose's Down Under** on Pender. This is a casual spot with good, reasonably priced food and friendly waiters (many from Australia). I like going here for a casual lunch with long-term clients and business associates.

4. **West Restaurant** on Granville. Although a bit out of the downtown core, it's well worth the trip. Small and offering excellent exotic West Coast food, this is a great place to go to really impress clients. The service is impeccable and the menu and wine selection is impressive.

5. **Imperial Chinese Restaurant** on Burrard. This is the best dim sum in downtown Vancouver. I take out of town guests here as many have never had dim sum and it is well worth the experience. The restaurant is big and open so it is, like all dim sum places, a bit loud. The food is good and the servers are attentive. You have to have dim sum if you're going for a schmooze lunch in Vancouver — we are the most Asian city in Canada, after all.

VANCOUVER BY EMPLOYMENT

By Occupation	Number Employed
Sales and service	263,770
Business, finance and administration	207,890
Trades, transport and equipment operators	130,110

Hydrogen

It was a BC government contract to build a hydrogen fuel-cell powered demonstration bus that launched a company and in turn created one of the biggest industry stirs of its time. When the bus was unveiled in June 1993 at Vancouver's Science World, it was no coincidence that Ballard used the opportunity to take his now Burnaby-based company (Ballard Power Systems Inc.) public.

The stock shot through the roof, making Ballard a wealthy man in the process. The automotive industry was literally beating a path to the Ballard door. Ballard spoke with certainty, telling anybody who would listen that his company would indeed produce a commercial product (emission-free proton exchange membrane fuel cells and systems that would be alternatives to internal combustion engines) for the automotive industry by the end of the decade. He told *Time* magazine that he expected fuel-cell cars would become economical by 2010 and that the internal-combustion engine would become obsolete.

There continue to be technical issues with widespread implementation of the technology. Indeed, Daimler and Ford bought Ballard's automotive fuel cell assets completely.

Ballard himself continued to believe. Almost right up until he died in August 2008, he worked with his new company, General Hydrogen, which again was working in hydrogen technology.

Ballard's most important gift to Vancouver was swagger. Here was the person considered the father of an industry, and he set up shop right here. He gave the province and a city a much needed boost of confidence. Despite being enticed to leave, he stayed. He received the Order of Canada in 1999 and in 2004 the Order of British Columbia.

Management	124,965
Social science, education, government, religion	85,980
Natural and applied sciences and related	75,150
Health	54,895
Processing, manufacturing and utilities	46,205
Art, culture, recreation and sport	42,595
Occupations unique to primary industry	18,350

Source: Statistics Canada.

EMPLOYMENT
(As of July 2008)
- Number of employed (full and part-time): 1.24 million
- Number of unemployed: 55,400
- Employment rate (as percentage of labour force): 95.7
- Employment rate (as percentage of population — based on 2007 population estimate of 2.25 million): 55.1

Source: BC Stats.

VANCOUVER'S GDP BY SECTOR
- Manufactured forest products: 22.7 percent
- Government (incl. public health and education): 14.6 percent
- Other manufacturing industries: 11 percent
- Construction: 8.8 percent
- Finance, insurance, real estate and leasing: 7.7 percent
- Transportation and storage: 6.5 percent
- Mining, quarrying and oil wells: 6.3 percent
- Business services: 3.9 percent
- Accommodation and food services: 3.2 percent
- Retail trade: 3.0 percent
- Communications and other utilities: 3.0 percent
- Logging and forestry: 2.1 percent
- Other: 7.1 percent

Source: Vancouver Board of Trade.

LEADING CANADIAN CITIES FOR HEAD OFFICE EMPLOYMENT AND PERCENTAGE OF CANADIAN TOTAL

- Toronto: 59,163 – 34 percent
- Montreal: 36,893 – 21 percent
- Calgary: 19,428 – 11 percent
- Vancouver: 11,938 – 7 percent
- Winnipeg: 6,890 – 4 percent

BUILDING PERMIT VALUES

City	Jan-Jun 2006	Jan-Jun 2007
Ottawa/Gatineau	$1.1 billion	$1.2 billion
Montreal	$2.87 billion	$3.2 billion
Calgary	$2.4 billion	$3.5 billion
Vancouver	$3.0 billion	$3.8 billion
Toronto	$5.0 billion	$6.2 billion

Source: Statistics Canada.

Did you know...

that Transport Canada estimates that the cost of traffic congestion in Metro Vancouver ranges between $700 million and $1.3 billion each year?

Did you know...

that in 1927 Charles Lindbergh refused to land in Vancouver, noting that "there is no fit field to land on." Soon after, the city decided to improve its landing facilities and in 1929 developers built Vancouver International Airport.

DOWNTOWN VANCOUVER

- Number of jobs: 145,000
- Number of stores: 9,139
- Number of dining spots/restaurants (not including take-outs or cafes): 375
- Number of movie theatres: 9
- Number of metred on-street parking spaces: 5,000
- Approximate number of off-street commercial parking spots: 53,000
- Number of hotel rooms: 12,242

OFFICE SPACE OCCUPANCY COSTS

Rate per square foot per year in selected cities, 2008

London, UK	$212.00
Tokyo, JP	$145.68
Manhattan, US	$62.00
Calgary	$53.51
Toronto	$52.80
Vancouver	**$41.01**
Ottawa	$38.45
Montreal	$30.08
Edmonton	$29.58
Asuncion, PY	$10.03

Source: Monster.ca

Did you know...

that Metro Vancouver was home to 67 percent of business incorporations in British Columbia in 2006?

Take 5 METRO VANCOUVER'S TOP FIVE
COMPANIES BY REVENUE

1. **Telus** (telecommunications) - $7.1 billion
2. **Jim Pattison Group** (media, signage, communications, automobiles) - $5.5 billion
3. **HY Louie** (wholesale grocers) - $4.0 billion
4. **Finning International** (heavy equipment) - $3.4 billion
5. **Teck Cominco** (mining)- $2.4 billion

Source: Business in Vancouver.

TAKING CARE OF BUSINESS (2007)
- Total number of businesses in Greater Vancouver: 193,632
- Number of businesses with between one and 19 employees: 77,888
- Number of businesses with between 20 and 49 employees: 6,376
- Businesses with no employees (run by self-employed owner): 105,394

Source: BC Statistics.

SMALL BUSINESS PER CAPITA
Vancouver has 38.4 small businesses per 1,000 people. Here's how some other major centres compare:
- Edmonton: 36.4
- Toronto: 28.2
- Ottawa: 27.1
- Montreal: 24.5

Source: Statistics Canada.

Did you know...

that 82 percent of Vancouver's workers say they would not accept a matching job offer somewhere else? On the other hand, nearly half of those working in the Toronto and Montreal would jump at the chance to relocate.

BANKRUPTCIES (2007)

	Consumer	vs 2006	Business	vs 2006
Vancouver (Proper)	871	-5.8%	49	-23.4%
BC	6,648	-5.2%	470	- 19.8%

Source: BC Statistics.

SELF-EMPLOYMENT (PER 1,000 PEOPLE)

- Calgary: 95.0
- **Vancouver: 93.7**
- Toronto: 76.9
- Edmonton: 75.1
- Ottawa: 69.3
- Montreal: 67.1

SELF-EMPLOYMENT GROWTH, 2002 - 2006

- Calgary: 22.8 percent
- Edmonton: 22.1 percent
- Montreal: 13.9 percent
- **Vancouver: 12.7 percent**
- Toronto: 9.9 percent
- Ottawa: 2.0 percent

Source: Alberta Economic Update.

Did you know...

that 82.4 percent of all jobs in Vancouver are service based?

They Said It

"The Vancouver Stock Exchange is to mining capital what Panama is to shipping — it's a place where you can always get a flag."
– Alan Young, Environmental Mining Council of British Columbia.

METRO VANCOUVER'S TOP FIVE
EMPLOYERS BY NUMBER OF EMPLOYEES

1. **Vancouver Coast Health Authority** – 24,000
2. **Fraser Health Authority** – 22,958
3. **University of British Columbia** – 16,179
4. **Vancouver Hospital & Health Sciences** – 10,000
5. **Provincial Health Services Authority** – 9,572

Source: Vancouver Economic Development.

TRANSPORTATION INFRASTRUCTURE
Riding the Rails

Three major railways link Vancouver to key Canadian, American and Mexican markets. Commercial railroad operators have "on-dock" access to Vancouver's shipping terminals, allowing for fast and more efficient movement of goods. Passengers can travel aboard the VIA Rail, Amtrak and Rocky Mountaineer Railtours services.

Roads

Vancouver, the westernmost mainland point for the Trans-Canada Highway, is linked by road to other major urban and business centres around the country. It is also connected to interstate routes and markets of the US by the five nearby border crossings. Transportation around Metro Vancouver is the charge of the Greater Vancouver Transportation Authority, Translink. As of 2007, $4 billion worth of road improvements were planned for the region.

Did you know...

that according to the American Association of Port Authorities, in 2006, Vancouver was the 41st busiest port in the world, the only Canadian port in the top 50 in the world?

Air

Vancouver International Airport is the second largest international passenger gateway on North America's West Coast and has the lowest landing fees in Canada. Located on Sea Island in the City of Richmond, immediately south of Vancouver, the airport is Canada's second busiest airport, and the second largest gateway on the West Coast of North America for international passengers. In 2007, it welcomed 17.5 million passengers, was the gateway for 226,234 tonnes of cargo, and had 274,410 runway takeoffs and landings in 2007.

Port of Vancouver

Vancouver's Port is Canada's largest and North America's second largest port in terms of foreign trade. The newly merged port's jurisdiction covers more than 600 km of coastline, borders 16 municipalities and boasts nearly 30 deep sea cargo terminals, two international cruise terminals and several short sea shipping terminals. The amalgamation has solidified the area as Canada's largest and busiest port, trading about $53 billion worth of goods and adding an estimated $6.3 billion to the local GDP in 2006.

Did you know...

that the Canadian restaurant chain, Boston Pizza, was started in Vancouver?

They Said It

"What is happening to our economy, indeed the world's economy, is that we are in an economic and cultural transformation that is as significant as any transformation in the past millennium. We are moving from an industrial economy to a knowledge economy—from an old economy to a new one."

– Dr. Jack Blaney of Simon Fraser University, speaking in 1998 to BC's first Business Summit.

EDUCATION SPINOFFS

- UBC generates 40,000 jobs and injects $6.3 billion into the Vancouver economy
- 8 percent of Vancouverites work in the education sector
- Teachers and professors comprise the third largest occupation group in the city
- UBC was Canada's first university to generate more than $100 million in cumulative licensing revenue from the sale of technologies and spin-off companies
- SFU has created more than 70 spin-off companies

TIMBER

It used to be that as the lumber industry went, so went the Vancouver economy. It is still a vital element of the economy here but its importance has diminished. In 2008, for example, forestry was in a serious slump. Mills have shut down across the province and venerable forest companies such as Pope and Talbot went into receivership. Indeed, PricewaterhouseCoopers declared 2008 the worst year ever for the BC forest sector.

Since the early 1990's, BC's coastal timber industry has largely stagnated. Rising costs, slumping demand for dimension lumber and the strong Canadian dollar have taken heavy tolls on earnings. Today,

Take 5 **TOP FIVE ORIGINS OF**
PORT OF VANCOUVER EXPORTS (2005)

1. **British Columbia** – 51 percent
2. **Alberta** – 26 percent
3. **Saskatchewan** – 15 percent
4. **Manitoba** – 4 percent
5. **Other provinces** – 4 percent

Source: Port of Vancouver.

forestry's share of GDP has declined to just over seven percent, and less than 15 with indirect and induced value-added.

By the Numbers — GDP Attributable to BC Forest Industries

- Forestry and logging: $3,272 million
- Wood product manufacturing: $4,902 million
- Pulp and paper manufacturing: $1,404 million
- Pulp, paper and paperboard mills: $1,280 million
- Converted paper product manufacturing: $124 million
- Total: $10,982 million
- Total BC GDP: $146,284 million

MINING

The mining industry can fairly be said to have begun when thousands of prospectors came to the area as gold was discovered along the shores of the Fraser River in the mid-nineteenth century. Exploration-oriented organizations and companies sprang up as a result, and there was a Mining Association of British Columbia as early as 1901. In short order the Vancouver Stock Exchange (1907) and the Association for Mineral Exploration of British Columbia (1912) followed.

British Columbia accounts for 17 percent of mining exploration in Canada. In 2007, investment in mineral exploration in the province reached an all time high of $416 million — a 1,300 percent increase over 2001. Greater Vancouver is home to more than 800 global mining and mineral and exploration companies.

DIGITAL MEDIA

Vancouver is home to more than 360 digital media companies operating in specialty areas such as interactive design, digital entertainment (gaming), digital film, animation and special effects, mobile content and E-learning.

Together they employ 10,000 people and generate $1.5 billion annually in sales. This success has been a direct result of a large creative workforce, proximity to the American West Coast, provincial tax breaks and the presence of several post-secondary institutions that specialize in digital media.

Firms such as giant Electronic Arts' studio, Disney, Nintendo, THQ, Vivendi/Activision have all set up shops here. EA's studio is the largest of its type in the world. There is also a strong symbiotic relationship with the established film and TV sector.

SUSTAINABILITY INDUSTRIES

Vancouver has long been associated with green industry leaders. In 2007, nearly half of Deloitte's "Technology Green 15 Companies" were centred in the city. Seventy percent of BC's clean technology sector — more than 800 companies which employ 12,000 employees — are based in Vancouver. When it comes to advanced energy solutions, Vancouver also fares well; 90 alternative energy companies (working in wind, solar and tidal power), with 3,000 employees and revenues of $750 million, operate in Vancouver.

TOURISM

Tourism is an industry on the rise in Vancouver. In 2007, 8,912,525 people visited the city, up 2.5 percent over 2006. In 2007, visitors spent $4,603,579,408, nearly $1.7 billion more than they spent in 2006.

Most visitors to Vancouver in 2007 were Canadians (5.4 million) followed by Americans (2.2 million). Another 768,913 came from Asia Pacific, 454,439 from Europe and the remaining 150,796 visitors were from other places internationally.

There are 24,000 hotel rooms in the area and as the Olympics loom this number is expected to grow by 2,500. In 2009, Vancouver's waterfront convention centre will triple to nearly 500,000 square feet to become Canada's largest convention centre with 70 meeting rooms and 300,000 square feet of exhibition space.

Between 2008 and 2015, it is projected that convention spending will double to nearly $1.2 billion million. The cruise industry is also important to Vancouver's economy. In 2007, 275 cruise ships docked in the city.

Weblinks

Vancouver Board of Trade
www.boardoftrade.com
The Vancouver Board of Trade has been supporting businesses of all sizes in the city for more than 100 years. Looking for ways to constantly promote trade, commerce and travel, the Board is a great sounding board for business in Vancouver.

Business in Vancouver
www.biv.com
Business in Vancouver magazine is the place to go to keep on top of what's going on business-wise, not only in Vancouver but also in the entire province of British Columbia.

Vancouver Economic Development
http://www.vancouvereconomic.com
Check out the online home of the Vancouver Economic Development Commission, which has all the information on how to do business in Vancouver and how to do it well.

Then and Now

Vancouver is one of Canada's youngest cities. By the time the Hudson's Bay Company opened a trading post at Fort Langley in 1827, the town that would eventually become known as Ottawa already had a school, the Bank of Montreal was ten years old and the *Halifax Gazette* — the continent's first newspaper — had been in print for 75 years.

In 1881, 22 years after New Westminster was established, Vancouver barely registered on the national census. Ten years later, it was the country's 12th most populous city. By the time of the next census in 1901 it had climbed to 10th place and to fourth by 1911.

HABLA ESPANOL?

Vancouverites came close to being Spanish. The Britishness that came to characterize the early city belies the fact that it was actually Spaniard José Maria Narvaez in 1791 who first laid eyes on what would become the Fraser River. In fact, nearly three centuries earlier Spain had claimed the entire West Coast of North America by the 1494 Treaty of Tordesillas.

England, already committed to the lucrative North American fur trade, was not about to let Spain claim the western trade and began plying the waters of British Columbia in the late 1780s. In 1789, the

Spanish navy seized English ships. When news of the seizure hit London in 1790, King George III ordered his navy to prepare for war. Knowing full well that war with England was one it could not win, Spain signed the Nootka Sound Convention in Madrid, relinquishing Spanish incontestable claims to the entire coast.

In 1791, Narvaez sailed past the mouth of the Fraser River, to the vicinity of present day Vancouver. It was a year later that Captain George Vancouver did the same. Britain saw the area had already been tagged by Spain and officials of the two nations met cordially near present day Point Grey. Together they continued exploring the area and in 1792 Captain Vancouver became the first European to sail up the Burrard Inlet.

POPULATION THEN AND NOW

1871: 1,419
1881: 9,991
1891: 18,229
1901: 27,198
1911: 60,104
1921: 60,879
1931: 246,593
1941: 275,353
1951: 344,833

They Said It

"Vancouver is, literally, one of the world's youngest cities."
— **Douglas Coupland, author of *City of Glass*.**

1961: 826,798 (CMA)
1971: 1,082,352 (CMA)
1976: 1,166,348 (CMA)
1981: 1,268,183 (CMA)
1991: 1,602,590 (CMA)
1996: 1,831,665 (CMA)
2001: 1,986,965 (CMA)
2006: 2,116,581 (CMA)

(Note: between 1961 and 1971, Point Grey and South Vancouver were annexed to Vancouver and the Greater Vancouver Regional District was incorporated, hence the immense population increases between those census years.)

Sources: Greater Vancouver Book; Statistics Canada; Greater Vancouver Regional Development.

GENDER (IM)BALANCE

Year	Men	Women
1881	5,540	4,451
1901	16,968	10,230
1921	34,867	26,012
1941	139,580	135,773
1961	189,504	195,018
1996	900,810	930,855
2001	972,730	1,014,235
2006	1,032,445	1,084,135

Source: Statistics Canada.

POPULATION BREAKDOWN

In 1869, the young territory of British Columbia had a population of 10,586. There were 2.5 men for every female, and 81 per cent of the population of 8,576 was Caucasian. Of the remaining 2,010 people, 462 were deemed to be of a "col'red race" and 1,458 were of the

Take 5 PAT REYNOLD'S TOP FIVE CHANGES
IN VANCOUVER OVER THE YEARS

Pat Reynolds was born in Chilliwack in 1939, but moved to Burnaby as a young girl. Her family later moved to Kitsilano and then Kerrisdale. Some of her fondest memories of Vancouver involved taking the historical interurban tram downtown to lunch at the old Woodward's Department Store followed by a movie. Her early career took her around the world but she returned to Vancouver in 1969 and in the late 1970s opened an antiques shop in Gastown.

1. There were no major high-rises on the city's horizon until after 1960. Vancouver was still a small town and the Sylvia Hotel in the West End displayed its neon rooftop sign advertising "Dine in the Sky." Upon my return to the city after working abroad, I noticed the many new high-rises, restaurants, shopping malls and increased population downtown. The building boom in the past ten or fifteen years has intensified these changes, especially in the West End, Coal Harbour, and Yaletown, as well as around the Granville and Cambie bridges.

2. Most of the wonderful neon signage on downtown Granville Street (movie theatres, restaurants, dress shops) has disappeared. In its glory days, this neon-lit street (fodder for many a postcard) was nick-named "The Great White Way" because of the dazzling neon signs.

"Chinese race." The Native population was not counted because, as the 1871 census explained, "details were wanting." However, figures produced in 1974 estimated a native population of between 20,000 and 50,000 for 1870s.

Source: 1871 Census of Canada.

3. The population growth has involved all cultures and has resulted in the proliferation of ethnic restaurants and world-class eateries in the past 20 years. People from every corner of the globe who have made Vancouver their home brought with them flavours, foods, fashions, customs and languages which have made Vancouver the fascinating culturally diverse city it has become.

4. Old style family neighbourhoods are being lost. The large middle class is decreasing as are affordable rentals, resulting in homelessness. Traditional neighbourhoods used to be places where everyone knew each other and helped each other if needed; people felt a lot safer and more comfortable.

5. There has been an upsurge in street pan-handling, crime to pay for drug addiction, gang warfare, marijuana grow-ops and an increase in burglar alarms. No more unlocked doors!

SELECT ETHNIC POPULATION OF VANCOUVER

	1901	1961	2006
Chinese and Japanese	2,840	25,519	406,879
English/Irish/Scot	20,080	491,084	753,215
French	598	30,507	137,270
German	871	51,056	203,715
Italian	203	18,300	76,345
Jewish	205	4,777	21,465
Scandinavian	452	45,140	113,270

Source: Statistics Canada.

No Cure for Gold Fever

In 1858, when the region around present-day Vancouver was still a forest home to a dusty trading post at Fort Langley, gold was discovered in the Fraser River Canyon. Word of the discovery traveled quickly and scores of California gold seekers rushed north.

About 30,000 miners turned this sparsely populated corner of the British Empire into a roaring town rivaled by no other in the region. Among them were the first of Vancouver's Chinese settlers, whose presence was not welcomed. Hardship was also the lot of First Nations people, who found it difficult to assert their rights in the face of gold fever.

Even when the rush moved inland and northward, Vancouver struck it rich as miners came in droves to the city to be outfitted and quickly became the economic capital of the region.

To this day mining (though no longer solely based on gold) remains very important to the Vancouver economy. The city is home to more mineral exploration companies than almost any other city in the world and in 2006 the province of British Columbia was responsible for nearly 20 percent of all mineral exploration in Canada.

TERMINUS CITY

It has been said that without the railway, there would be no Vancouver. When Canada came courting and as BC laid out her terms for Confederation in 1870 (the year before it joined), at the top of the list was the construction of a railway linking British Columbia and Winnipeg. Canada, eager to have the West Coast colony, obliged and by the 1880s the railway had been extended to BC.

In August 1884, William Cornelius Van Horne, Vice President of the Canadian Pacific Railway, traveled to BC to choose the ultimate western terminus for the railroad. While many lobbied for Port Moody,

Komagata Maru Incident

In 1914, the Japanese-owned ship *Komagata Maru* sailed out of Hong Kong. Aboard were 376 Indians seeking better lives in Vancouver. No more welcomed than Chinese or Japanese immigrants, Indians faced discriminatory immigration rules and the provincial government asserted that Indians not arriving direct from India would not be allowed to enter.

This law was tested when 38 Sikhs were allowed entry in 1913 on the grounds that ships at that time offered continuous passage from India. When the *Komagat Maru* sailed into Burrard Inlet on May 23, 1914, the government was, however, determined to keep them out.

Passengers were detained on board for two months before the full ship was turned around and sent back to India. The Indian government received the would-be immigrants with suspicion, which resulted in a shootout and a number of deaths.

On May 23, 2008, on the sad event's 94th anniversary, the government of British Columbia unanimously passed Motion 62, formally apologizing for the incident. This action followed by just a few days an apology from the federal government. The Conservative government of Stephen Harper has pledged $2.5 million for the creation of a *Komagata Maru* memorial.

> "This is destined to be a great city, perhaps the greatest in Canada. We must see to it that it has a name commensurate with its dignity and importance, and Vancouver it shall be, if I have the ultimate decision."
> – William Cornelius Van Horne of the CPR, who named the city.

Van Horne selected the town of Granville, in part because of its deep harbour. Van Horne also proposed a name change. A connoisseur of history, Van Horne was set on changing the name of Granville to Vancouver, in honour of the famed British seaman.

In February of 1887, the first CPR train arrived in Vancouver and on May 23 of that year the first transcontinental passenger train reached the city. Thanks to CPR funds and initiative, the newly-named railway town was home to not just to a train station, but shops, a hotel and an opera house, all built by the CPR.

THANK YOU, MR. HAMILTON

Lauchlan Hamilton, CPR land commissioner and one of the first aldermen in the city of Vancouver, had an important role in the city's geographical history. In 1885, Hamilton mapped out the area of today's downtown Vancouver, naming its streets. Despite his fervent wish to create a straight grid outline, outrageous forests and a few stubborn landowners forced him to settle for the almost grid we know today.

Did you know...

that the person who drove the last spike in the Canadian Pacific Railway on November 7, 1885 at Eagle Pass Vancouver was rail-road financier Donald Smith?

Forty years after he completed the survey, Hamilton lamented: "I cannot say that I am proud of the original planning of Vancouver. The work, however, was beset with many difficulties."

Source: The History of Metropolitan Vancouver.

A Chinese Hero

In the early twentieth century, Chinese men who had immigrated to Canada would, on rare occasions, make the expensive journey back to China to see their families (for whom they could not afford the immigration head tax). Sometimes decades passed between visits. This made Vancouver a lonely place for Chinese men who, far from home, were treated as second class citizens. By the late 1940s, however, Chinese immigrants were able to bring their spouses, young children and elderly parents to join them in Vancouver. These changes were due in large part to the efforts of Wong Foon Sein.

Born in China around 1900, Wong was one of the first five Chinese people to attend the University of British Columbia. Wong became well known in his community as a court interpreter in 1924, the year following the 1923 Chinese Immigration Act that tightened restrictions on would-be migrants from China.

In 1937, Wong was put in charge of public relations for the Chinese Benevolent Association's Aid-to-China program. He worked passionately to heighten awareness of the situation of the Chinese in Canada. Because of his fluency in both Chinese and English, he was hired by government during World War II.

At war's end Wong moved to Victoria to work at a Chinese daily and took up the cause of voting rights for Canadian Chinese. In a long fought battle, Wong was instrumental in the 1947 repeal of the offensive 1923 Chinese Immigration Act. This change in law paved the way for the Chinese of Canada to become citizens with full rights, including the franchise. After his retirement in the 1960s Wong remained an active and outspoken proponent of equal Chinese participation in a multicultural Canadian society.

FRANCHISE

In 1917 when women were finally allowed to vote in municipal elections, the right was not extended to men or women of Oriental or Aboriginal descent. As World War II raged, the issue of Asian enfranchisement came to a head. Although they were subject to conscription and although many served voluntarily in the Canadian forces, only military enlistees — and not civilians of Asian origin — were granted the vote in 1945. After much pressure, particularly from the Chinese Canadian community, all Canadians of Asian descent were finally granted the federal franchise in 1948. The provincial vote followed a year later.

HIGHER EDUCATION

In 1877, British Columbia's Superintendent of Education proposed a provincial university. A 13-year fight to have legislation passed was followed by years of back-and-forth between Vancouver and Victoria over which should host the university.

Finally, in 1899, Vancouver High School, with the help of McGill University in Montreal, started Vancouver College, later renamed the McGill University College of British Columbia. Although an improvement, this school still required students to finish degrees elsewhere.

In 1907, the province passed the University Endowment Act allowing the sale of provincial crown land to raise funds for the British Columbia University. A year later, the University Act established the university as a non-sectarian and co-ed institution. By 1910, Point Grey near Vancouver was chosen as the site for the new school and construction began in 1914.

Did you know...

that in 1919 the Rex Theatre — which used to stand on West Hastings — charged $0.10 to see a movie in the afternoon? The price of admission rose to $0.15 for evening shows, except for children, who paid five cents admission all day long.

World War I temporarily halted construction and more than 300 students attended a temporary campus during the war. At war's end, enrollment swelled and students demanded a new school with a 1922 protest and 56,000-name petition. Student resolve paid off and fewer than three years later, students were settling in at their new Point Grey campus.

As course offerings expanded, so did the campus. In 1958 the university launched the UBC Development Fund — making history as the first Canadian university to solicit public contributions. The fund worked as private contributors and government netted the school $35 million.

Today UBC boasts four campuses across the province and has 250,000 alumni in 120 countries, among them such famous Canadians such as Nobel laureate Robert Mundell, former Prime Ministers John Turner and Kim Campbell, author Pierre Berton, athlete and fundraiser Rick Hanssen and opera singers Ben Heppner and Judith Forst.

VOTERS' RIGHTS

Vancouver's first City Council in 1886, like that of today, consisted of a Mayor and ten Aldermen elected at large. To qualify for a position, a candidate had to reside in Vancouver, be a male British subject aged at least 21 years old, and own $1,000 worth of real estate or $2,000 worth of leased property. To cast a ballot in the city's first election, voters — male or female —had to be 21 years old or older, a freeholder, householder for at least six months before the election, pre-emptor or leaseholder, also for six months.

Source: City of Vancouver.

Did you know...

that the University of British Columbia imposed its first tuition on students in 1920, five years after it first opened its doors? The annual cost: $40.

RADIO WAVES

Vancouver has been home to many firsts in the world of radio. In 1922, the *Vancouver Province* newspaper introduced the new medium, broadcasting its first radio newscast to listeners from Vancouver all the way to High River, Alberta. The station, CKCD, entertained and informed Vancouverites until 1940.

A year after CKCD hit the airwaves, mayoral candidate W.R. Owen became the first candidate to campaign on radio. Perhaps the most important point in Vancouver's radio history was the inauguration of CNRV in 1925, the first radio network in North America. The broadcasts began from a studio in the Vancouver station of Canadian National Railroad for listeners riding its trains all across the country. CNRV operated until 1932 when it became the backbone of the Canadian Radio Broadcasting Commission, the predecessor for the Canadian Broadcasting Corporation.

Source: Vancouver Radio Museum; Canadian Communications Foundation; Alberta Provincial Archives.

TRANSPORTATION TIMELINE

1873: The *Eleanora* becomes the first motorized ferry service across the Burrard Inlet.

1887: The Canadian Pacific Railway train arrives in Vancouver.

1889: The first of three Granville Street bridges is built.

1899: Stanley Park Stables, the city's only taxi service, boasts 86 horses and 40 rigs.

1899: First crank car is seen on Vancouver streets.

1904: The first gas-powered car arrives in the city.

1902: Vancouver's (and Canada's) first gas station opens on Smyth Street.

1908: First bus service for tourists commences in Stanley Park.

1914: Bus service begins between New Westminster and Aldergrove.

1915: Bus service begins between New Westminster and White Rock.

1915: Vancouver gets its first sightseeing bus and taxi service.

1916: West Vancouver gets municipal bus service.

1922: Bus service begins between Vancouver and Port Moody and Port Coquitlam.

1925: The first of two Second Narrows bridges is built to span the water between Vancouver and North Vancouver.

1938: The Lions Gate Bridge is completed.

1948: Electric buses start transporting Vancouverites.

1948: Burnaby gets its first bus service.

1955: Vancouver's last streetcar is taken off the road.

1959: The George Massey Tunnel opens, allowing cars to drive under the Fraser River.

1985: The SkyTrain begins operations ahead of WorldExpo '86.

2001: Vancouver experiences a four-month transit strike.

2008: Vancouver transit expands in preparation for the 2010 Olympic Games.

Source: The History of Metropolitan Vancouver.

BEFORE THE BRIDGE

Before the Lions Gate Bridge was built in 1938, people from West Vancouver traveled downtown by ferry. In 1909, the first regular ferry service, the West Vancouver Ferry Company, opened for business and in two years had a fleet of two.

In 1912, the company was sold to the newly minted municipality of West Vancouver for $6,000. Under municipal control, the service expanded, adding more ferries to the fleet. A journey across the harbour took 25 minutes and cost 10 cents, a fare that later raised to fifteen cents.

Although the advent of the bridge ended the service, it was revived briefly during World War II when security concerns closed the bridge.

Source: West Vancouver Museum and Archives.

THE MILLIONAIRES

Founded in 1911, the Vancouver Millionaires were part of the professional Pacific Coast Hockey Association. They played out of the Denman Street Arena, which had a seating capacity of 10,500, and at the time was only one of two Canadian arenas with artificial ice.

The Vancouver Millionaires vied for the Stanley Cup no fewer than five times between their incarnation and 1926, winning the cup once in 1915 when they beat the Ottawa Senators, becoming the first western team to win the prize. The Millionaires would never win the cup again, but in 1917-18, 1920-21 and 1921-22 they made it to the finals.

Did you know...

that Vancouver was home to Canada's first drive-through restaurant? In 1926, Nat Bailey opened his first hotdog stand to serve motorists at Look Out Point on SW Marine Drive. From these humble beginnings rose the famous White Spot restaurant chain, now 60 stores strong.

They Said It

> "They played the clubs in Vancouver, but they couldn't stay in a [high-class] hotel or frequent places because of their colour, so they'd come to our place."
>
> — Jane Reifel, daughter of George Jr., recalling the jazz greats who played at her family's Vancouver mansion.

REIFEL FAMILY

Born in Bavaria in 1869, Henry Reifel came to Vancouver by way of the USA in 1888. A brewer by trade, Henry continued this livelihood in Vancouver, eventually opening Canadian Brewing and Malting (at 11th and Yew) in 1908, and later amalgamating it into a larger conglomerate called Vancouver Breweries.

Reifel's sons George and Harry had the misfortune of taking over the family business at the height of prohibition. As prohibition enveloped the west coasts of Canada (1917-1920) and the United States (1920-1933), the enterprising sons turned to rum-running. The family-owned vessel, the *Malahat*, became a fixture off the West Coast. When Canada went "wet" again, Henry and sons returned to legal booze production, re-opening the Vancouver brewery and expanding with the B.C. Distilleries Company in New Westminster.

Standing as a testament to the family's business acumen was the 20,782 square foot Casa Mia, a mansion built by George Sr. on Southwest Marine Drive in 1932 (sold by the family in the 1960s). In the 1940s heyday of jazz, George Jr. turned the home into the centre of Vancouver's jazz scene, hosting the likes of Louis Armstrong and Duke Ellington at parties.

Did you know...

> that Vancouver's first streetlights began to light the night on Hastings Street on December 18, 1929?

Take 5 COST OF FIVE THINGS
IN VANCOUVER IN 1924

1. **Prime rib roast:** $0.10/lb
2. **Three pounds of butter:** $1.35
3. **Shaving cream:** $0.23
4. **Salmon steaks:** $0.30/lb
5. **Lard,** 5lb pail: $0.79

THE GREAT DEPRESSION

Vancouver did not escape the "Dirty Thirties." Vancouverites, like people across the nation, found themselves out of work and families' resources stretched to the breaking point.

Although 1930s Vancouver prices seem inexpensive today — $2.49 for a pair of women's shoes, eight cents for a can of Campbells Soup, nine cents for bathroom tissue and seven cents for two heads of lettuce — these ordinary things were out of reach of many.

A federal solution to the crisis, the creation of Relief Camps for unemployed single men, was inadequate and in the mid-1930s men in these camps, fed up with camp conditions and poor compensation, formed the Relief Camp Workers Union and launched a strike. In the spring of 1935, Vancouver strikers noisily voiced their anger.

When Ottawa failed to respond, the men decided to take their grievances to straight to Ottawa. On June 3, strikers left Vancouver on their famed On To Ottawa Trek, picking up supporters as they traveled east. The men never did get their desired meeting. In Regina later that month, the strikers clashed violently with police and the trek ended.

Did you know...

that at the start of the Great Depression, Vancouver had the highest level of unemployment in the country at 28 percent?

They Said It

> "I speak for Members on all sides of the House today in offering to Japanese Canadians the formal and sincere apology of this Parliament for those past injustices against them, against their families and against their heritage, and our solemn commitment and undertaking to Canadians of every origin the such violations will never again in this country be countenanced or repeated."
>
> – Right Honourable Brian Mulroney, 1988, offering the federal government's apology to interned Japanese-Canadians.

WORLD WAR II

Like the rest of the world, Vancouver was rattled by World War II. By 1941, the city was deep into 'war mode,' hoping for the best and preparing for the worst.

On May 22 of that year the whole city went dark as it had its first practice blackout and in early December another such blackout—this one in the immediate aftermath of the bombing of Pearl Harbor—even saw an electric flame on a WWI memorial in Stanley Park snuffed out. Before Christmas, school children and most of the rest of the general public were learning how to use gas masks as they went about their daily business.

Source: The History of Metropolitan Vancouver; Discover Vancouver.

INTERNMENT

Anti-Asian sentiment, long woven into the fabric of Vancouver, reached the boiling point during World War II. Tensions between Vancouver's Japanese and non-Japanese population rose as Japan's actions increasingly antagonized the Allies. Japan's bombing of Pearl Harbor in December 1941 raised anxiety in Vancouver and sealed the fate of Japanese people living in Vancouver.

Now at war with Japan and facing public demands to counter an

171

"*The government has concurred in the recommendations [of the Bird Commission] and money has been made available to meet the claims. In carrying out the recommendations of Mr. Justice Bird we feel we have discharged our obligation to both the Japanese Canadians and to the general public.*"
– Prime Minister Louis St. Laurent, following compensation payments to Japanese Canadians who lost property during the internment years.

undefined "Japanese threat" that escalated into wartime hysteria, the RCMP confiscated and sold Japanese fishing boats, vehicles and electronics. Japanese were barred from the coast, subject to a dusk-to-dawn curfew and were fired from their jobs.

As the war with Japan continued, a chorus demanded the internment of the Japanese. On February 27, 1942, the Canadian government gave into these demands and announced plans to remove the Japanese from the BC coast. More than 22,000 Japanese-born, aliens and Canadian citizens alike, were ordered to pack a single suitcase and sent to the BC interior or further eastward. Their homes and possessions were sold.

Only in 1949 were the restrictions lifted. At that time a commission was created to answer the claims of Japanese people who had lost property during the internment years. In 1950 the commission awarded $1.3 million to 1,434 Japanese in compensation, but the award fell short of an apology. The country's Japanese would have to wait until 1988 when Prime Minister Brian Mulroney's government officially apologized for their internment.

THE CANADIAN

The 1950s saw another rail milestone in Vancouver when the CPR introduced the Canadian, a thoroughly modern streamline train that would cross the Canadian continent. The trains (there would eventually be a half dozen in operation) featured the now famous glassed dome cars which allowed passengers spectacular panoramic views of the Canadian countryside during their 71 hour jaunt between Montreal and Vancouver.

Designed as a lavish way to travel in the prosperous post-war era, the Canadian featured spacious sleeping quarters and top notch dining (a sirloin steak cost $3.00 and apple pie, 30 cents). In 1978, VIA Rail took over the service. Today's version of the Canadian runs between Toronto and Vancouver.

Weblinks

Vancouver Historical Society

www.vancouver-historical-society.ca

For more than 70 years, this group has been preserving and promoting the history of Vancouver, including its historic buildings and monuments.

Vancouver Museum

www.vanmuseum.bc.ca/index.htm

This online home for the Vancouver Museum offers information on past, current and upcoming exhibits and the window each of them open to Vancouver's past and present.

The History of Metropolitan Vancouver

www.vancouverhistory.ca/

Almost no site available offers a glimpse into Vancouver's past like this one, operated by Chuck Davis, a local Vancouver historian who is putting together a comprehensive book by the same name.

Politics

Like all early frontier towns, Vancouver was a town of hustlers and new beginnings. Lumber and gold brought the initial newcomers, but later the railway and natural resources would be the draw. In 1886, when the first Canadian Pacific Railway train rolled into the newly chosen western terminus, it assured Vancouver's rise in economic and political importance.

The railway brought with it speculators and grafters, but it also brought a steady stream of hardworking newcomers who would form the backbone of the new community. Early political interests were largely guided by an emerging business class.

Since the mid-1940s, municipal government in the city has been dominated by the centre-right Non-Partisan Association (NPA). The current Vancouver mayor Sam Sullivan was elected mayor of Vancouver in November 2005, bringing the NPA to power again.

Different political ideologies aside, political consensus has emerged in Greater Vancouver surrounding some important issues, such as parkland protection, the value of 'green' technology and a pressing desire to solve rampant drug problems in the Downtown Eastside.

They Said It

CITY GOVERNMENT

Vancouver's government consists of the Vancouver City Council, the Board of Parks and Recreation and the School Board, all of which are elected. The council is made up of the mayor and ten councilors, while the parks and school boards have seven and nine members each, respectively. Municipal elections are held across BC every three years on the third Sunday of November and representatives are elected for three-year terms.

The 27 members of Vancouver's municipal government are elected using an 'at large' system, meaning that voters cast ballots for all ten councilors, rather than just the one who will represent the area in which they live.

In 2004, Vancouverites voted on whether or not to uphold the at-large system or to replace it with a ward system with 14 proposed wards. The majority chose to keep the at-large system.

Source: City of Vancouver.

They Said It

GREATER VANCOUVER

Unlike many urban centres in Canada, Vancouver and its surrounding municipalities have not amalgamated. The 21 municipalities are, however, legally part of the Greater Vancouver Regional District (now called Metro Vancouver) and form one electoral area. There is also a

Take 5   MAYOR SAM SULLIVAN'S TOP FIVE
THINGS ABOUT BEING MAYOR OF VANCOUVER

A skiing accident left Sam Sullivan a quadriplegic at age 19. Sullivan was first elected to Vancouver's City Council in 1993, and twelve years later was elected mayor. Sullivan will be a one-term mayor. In June 2008 his Non-Partisan Association party narrowly endorsed another candidate, Peter Ladner, for the 2008 electoral contest.

1. Vancouver is a great place to learn languages and celebrate diversity. Every year since its inception in 1886, more than 50 percent of Vancouver residents have come from somewhere else. The city is constantly invigorated with new people.

2. Vancouver is the only big city in North America without a freeway running through it.

3. The downtown peninsula of Vancouver has a higher density of population than Manhattan. This has contributed to our quality of life and reduced our environmental footprint. We are the definition of a clean and green city. You can't beat the fresh air during a nice evening stroll along the Stanley Park seawall.

4. Because almost all of Canada's major urban centres have amalgamated their municipalities, their politics are dominated by suburban priorities. In that sense, Vancouver is really one of the only truly urban municipalities left in Canada. Our values are distinctly urban in nature.

5. We are recognized as an international innovator regarding compassionate drug policy. We are home to North America's only safe injection site for drug users so we can get them off the streets and back alleys, and into the care of medical professionals.

1. **Philip Owen**, 9 years
2. **Louis Taylor**, 8 years
3. **F. J. Hume**, 7 years
4. **Gordon Campbell**, 7 years
5. **Michael Harcourt**, 6 years

Source: City of Vancouver.

single seat for all unincorporated land, which includes the University Endowment Lands and Barnston Island.

The Greater Vancouver Regional District Board (GVRD) is made up of elected officials from each of the 21 municipalities (with population being the determining factor when deciding both how many board members each municipality sends to the table and how much each official's vote is worth). For every 20,000 people in a municipality, an official gets one vote to a maximum of five for municipalities with populations of 100,000 or more.

Source: Greater Vancouver Regional Development, World Bank.

They Said It

"It was based on sport. The Austrian bid was cultural and the Korean bid was too political. I think [Vancouver] was a good choice. They were the most sports-related bid."
– Roland Baar, International Olympic Committee member from Germany
on Vancouver's winning bid for the 2010 Olympic Games
(as reported in the *New York Times*, July 3, 2003.)

Did you know...

that each of Vancouver's ten City Councilors serves as Deputy Mayor on a monthly, rotating basis?   .

Mayors of Vancouver

Term	Name	Profession
1886 - 1887	M. A. MacLean	Realtor
1888 - 1891	David Oppenheimer	Entrepreneur
1892 - 1893	Frederick Cope	Builder
1894	R. A. Anderson	Realtor
1895 - 1896	Henry Collins	Merchant
1897	William Templeton	Butcher
1898 - 1900	James F. Garden	Engineer
1901	Thomas Owen Townley	Lawyer
1902 - 1903	Thomas Fletcher Neelands	Flour / Seed Merchant
1904	William J. McGuigan	Doctor / Lawyer
1905 - 1906	Frederick Buscombe	Glass Merchant
1907 - 1908	Alexander Bethune	Shoe Merchant
1909	Charles S. Douglas	Realtor
1910 - 1911	Louis Denison Taylor	Writer / Editor
1912	James Findlay	Businessman
1913 - 1914	Truman Smith Baxter	Business Administrator
1915	Louis Denison Taylor	Writer / Editor
1916 - 1917	Malcolm Peter McBeath	Politician
1918 - 1921	Robert Henry Gale	Realtor
1922 - 1923	Charles Edward Tisdal	Politician
1924	William Reid Owen	Realtor / Insurance Agent
1925 - 1928	Louis Denison Taylor	Writer and Editor
1929 - 1930	William Harold Malkin	Wholesale Grocer
1931 - 1934	Louis Denison Taylor	Writer / Editor
1935 - 1936	Gerald Grattan McGeer	Lawyer
1937 - 1938	George Clark Miller	Politician
1939 - 1940	James Lyle Telford	Doctor
1941 - 1946	Jonathan Webster Cornett	Shoe Merchant
1947	Gerald Grattan McGeer	Lawyer
1948	Charles Jones	Politician
1949 - 1950	Charles Edwin Thompson	Teacher / Rancher
1951 - 1958	Frederick Hume	Philanthropist
1959 - 1962	A. Thomas Alsbury	Teacher
1963 - 1966	William Rathie	Tax Accountant
1967 - 1972	Tom Campbel	Lawyer / Developer
1973 - 1976	Arthur Phillips	Investment Analyst
1977 - 1980	Jack Volrich	Lawyer
1980 - 1986	Michael Harcourt	Politician
1986 - 1993	Gordon Campbell	Developer
1993 - 2002	Philip Owen	Politician
2002 - 2005	Larry Campbell	Law Enforcement
2005 - 2008	Sam Sullivan	Politician

THE VANCOUVER CHARTER

Unlike other municipalities in BC that are governed by the Local Government Act, the City of Vancouver is governed by the Vancouver Charter, a provincial statute that gives the city more freedom than others to determine how it operates.

The statute authorizes the city to pass laws on things such as land use, the buying and selling of property, tax collection, debt management and grant distribution.

THE CURRENT ADMINISTRATION

- Mayor: Sam Sullivan
- Party: Non-Partisan Association
- Date sworn in: November 2005
- Number of Councillors: 10
- Number of School Board Trustees: 9
- Number of Park Commissioners: 7
- Number of NPA members in municipal government: 16
- Number of COPE members in municipal government: 7
- Number of VIV members in municipal government: 1
- Voting age: 18

Residency: One must be a resident of BC for at least six months immediately before the General Voting Day, and be registered as a voter for the electoral district, either before the election or at the time of voting.

Source: City of Vancouver.

Did you know...

that the annual salary of the Mayor of Vancouver in 2007 was $122,358.34? City Councilors earned less than half that amount — $53,902.35 — for the same period, as well as $2,243.23 for each month they served as Deputy Mayor.

They Said It

"I declare this thing open — whatever it is."
– HRH Prince Philip, on the opening of a
new annex at Vancouver City Hall.

PARTIES

Vancouver is home to a number of civic-level political parties:

1. Coalition of Progressive Electors (COPE)
2. Green Party of Vancouver
3. Vancouver Civic Non-Partisan Association
4. Nude Garden Party
5. Vancouver's Interest Party
6. Vision Vancouver
7. Work Less Party

Source: City of Vancouver.

GOVERNMENT DOUGH: WHERE VANCOUVER GETS ITS CASH

In 2006 the City of Vancouver had a balanced budget of $813.3 million. The largest single source of cash came from $516.3 million in property taxes.

- Total revenue: $813 billion
- Property taxes: 63 percent
- User fees and sundry revenues: 19 percent
- Utility fees: 17 percent
- Transfer from reserves/funds: 1 percent

They Said It

"[He] was warm-hearted, liberal-minded gentleman, and possessed magnetic qualities that compelled affection."
– Vancouver Daily World, obituary of M.A. MacLean, Vancouver's first
mayor, as reported in the *Dictionary of Canadian Biography*.

SPENDING THE DOUGH: WHERE VANCOUVER SPENDS ITS CASH

In 2006, Vancouver's single largest expense was the Vancouver Police Department, which cost a total of $175.1 million, or nearly 22 percent of the total budget.

- Total expenditures: $813 billion
- Police: 22 percent
- Utilities: 21 percent
- Parks and Recreation: 11 percent

 PATRICK SMITH'S TOP FIVE
'GREAT VANCOUVERITES' IN POLITICS/PUBLIC POLICE/PUBLIC LIFE

Patrick J. Smith, Ph.D, LSE is Director of the Institute of Governance Studies and Professor (and past Chair) of Political Science at Simon Fraser University, where he has taught since 1982. He has also served on the boards of the Canadian Political Science Association, the Institute of Public Administration of Canada and the British Columbia Political Studies Association. Smith's many articles, books and reviews include those written on the politics and government of Vancouver.

1. **Dr. David Suzuki**, academic, public broadcaster, environmentalist. Suzuki epitomizes the best of Vancouver and BC and its contributions to local, national and global sustainability, from Greenpeace to saving salmon.

2. **Mike Harcourt**, lawyer, civil society activist, former Vancouver Mayor (1980-1986), GVRD Chair, provincial Opposition leader (1986-1991), Premier of BC (1991-1996), member of enviro/economy roundtable for federal government. His major accomplishment was re-adding the province to First Nations deliberations. He did most of the work on governmental side in the Nisga'a Treaty, BC's and Canada's first 'modern' treaty. Via the World Urban Forum he adds to thinking about urban life and global sustainability.

- Fire: 10 percent
- Engineering (streets, transportation, electrical and administration): 7 percent
- General administration: 7 percent
- Debt: 6 percent
- Community services: 6 percent
- Library: 4 percent
- Contingency and transfers: 3 percent
- Civic grants: 2 percent
- Civic theatres: 1 percent

3. **Gordon Campbell**, businessman, former Vancouver Mayor (1986-1992), Greater Vancouver Regional Development Chair, provincial Opposition leader (1993-2001), Premier of BC since 2001. During his second term he has sought reconciliation with BC's First Nations/Aboriginal peoples.

4. **Vancouver's Coast Salish peoples**. Vancouver is in the traditional territories of the Skwxwu7mesh, Xwmethkwyiem and Tseilwaututh First Nations. Together with their other First Nations in Greater Vancouver and on the Lower Mainland, these groups assisted early non-Aboriginal settlers and have persisted over hundreds of years of colonial rule. They continue to form Vancouver's closest connection to this land and its sustainability.

5. **Dr. H. Peter Oberlander,** OC, Founder of UBC's School of Community and Regional Planning/Centre for Human Settlements, first federal 'deputy minister' for Urban Affairs, teacher, scholar, UN Habitat to World Urban Forum catalyst, federal advisor, citizenship court judge. He is one of Vancouver's pre-eminent urbanists and is known across the globe.

OPERATING BUDGETS APPROVED BY VANCOUVER CITY COUNCIL
2004: $738 million
2005: $773 million
2006: $813 million
2007: $848 million

DEBT
At the end of 2006, the City of Vancouver was in debt to the tune of $505.9 million, down 21.6 percent from $645.1 million at the end of 2005.

Source: The City of Vancouver.

PROPERTY TAXES AND UTILITY COSTS (2007)
Based on a sample house as defined as a 25 to 30 year-old detached 3-bedroom bungalow with a main floor area of 1,200 square feet, finished full basement and a double car garage, on a 6,000 square foot lot. Utility charges include telephones, power, water, sewer, land drainage and garbage collection.

Ottawa	$4,659
Toronto	$4,624
Saskatoon	$4,487
Vancouver	$4,216
St. John's	$4,082
Calgary	$3,708
Montreal	$3,644
Halifax	$3,402

Source: City of Edmonton.

FIRST LADY OF VANCOUVER POLITICS
During the 1890s, the women of British Columbia were allowed to vote in municipal elections as long as they paid property taxes (a caveat that disenfranchised many women). In 1908, amidst protest, this right to vote was rescinded. After years of hard work, ignored petitions and a ref-

The Real-life DaVinci

Life has taken Larry Campbell in some strange directions. The plain-spoken former Hamilton steelworker turned RCMP officer arrived in Vancouver in 1969, joining the drug squad four years later. In 1981, he established the City of Vancouver's first District Coroner's Office. In 1996, he became the Chief Coroner for the province of British Columbia.

To most people that is a career, but a chance meeting with Vancouver writer/producer Chris Haddock changed all that. Campbell invited Haddock to speak at an international forensics science convention about the role of a medical examiner he had created for a U.S. pilot he was pitching.

What Campbell didn't know was that Haddock had earned his keep for many years on the streets of Vancouver as a busker. Both men had unusual understanding of the people and the streets of Vancouver. It was a ready friendship and it turns out a match made in heaven.

Haddock created *Da Vinci's Inquest* based on Campbell. (Campbell even served as a consultant for the show.) The show went on to become one of the most successful and longest running dramas in the history of Canadian television. In Vancouver, it elevated Campbell to the status of folk hero.

In 2002, Campbell ran for mayor on a platform that called for, among other things, the opening of Vancouver's (and one of North America's) first safe-injection site. He won in a landslide. Although his period in office would be characterized by internal party bickering, a safe injection site opened in 2003 and Campbell also saw to it that the Vancouver Police Department increase the number of officers to the downtown Eastside.

What Campbell also brought to the mayor's office was colour. He was often seen wearing a long trench coat. Campbell reignited interest in municipal politics.

Although Campbell announced he was going to run for mayor again in 2005, he withdrew after Prime Minister Paul Martin offered him Senate seat. In the Senate, he is the chair of the Liberal Urban Caucus and continues to be active in civic affairs and particularly that of Vancouver.

erendum, the municipal vote was returned to women in 1917. That same year women got the provincial vote and the federal franchise.

In 1917, teacher Mary Ellen Smith ran as an independent MLA for a Vancouver by-election, seeking the seat of her recently deceased husband, Ralph. She won and would go on to become the first female member of the BC legislature and the first female cabinet member of the British Empire.

Until her death in 1933, Smith was a tireless supporter of women's rights and advancement, including advocating the province's first Mother's Pensions and Female Minimum Wage Acts.

Sources: Marianopolis College website; Canadian Encyclopedia.

MAYOR PRIMER

- Number of mayors who have served since 1886: 38
- First Non-Partisan Association mayor: Jonathan Webster Cornett, 1941-1946
- First TEAM (The Electors' Action Movement — now defunct) mayor: Art Phillips, 1973-1976
- First Coalition of Progressive Electors (COPE) mayor: Larry Campbell, 2002-2005
- Youngest mayor: Fred Cope, 32 years old when elected, 1892-1893
- Longest-serving mayor: Philip Owen, 9 years
- First Vancouver-born mayor: William George Rathie, 1963-1966
- Number of mayors born outside of British Columbia: 32

Did you know...

that two mayors of Vancouver have also served as its premier? Michael Harcourt, mayor between 1980-1986, was also NDP Premier of BC between 1991 and 1996 while Gordon Campbell, mayor between 1986-1993, is the current Liberal premier of BC, a post he has held since 2001.

MORE FEMALE FIRSTS

Senator Mobina Jaffer, who is of East Indian descent, was born in Uganda where she lived before moving to attend school in the UK and Canada. She eventually became the first East Indian woman to practice law in British Columbia and, in 2001, became the first African-

Fire Trap

Anything could happen in the early history of Vancouver. A 42-year-old Scotsman named Malcolm MacLean had been in town four months when the powers that be had him running for mayor.

Before he got to Vancouver, he had spent three years teaching in Ontario, worked for Cunard in New York and set up a wholesale company in Winnipeg. He was on his way to Hawaii for another venture, when the family took a turn for a tiny place called Granville.

Granville may only have had 600 people, but she was going to be the western terminus, which almost automatically elevated her importance.

MacLean was up against Richard Alexander who was manager of the Hastings Sawmill and had lived in the area for more than ten years. MacLean won by just 17 votes (his election was challenged by Alexander). For his part, MacLean accused Alexander of bringing his Chinese workers to vote, but it didn't matter because they were denied anyway.

One of the first orders of business for MacLean was dealing with potential fire problems in what was essentially a lumber town. The new council members agreed and had one on order. It would do little good, however, because on June thirteenth a scrap fire spread through town and every building was reduced to ashes.

MacLean and his family lost all their possessions, but like the rest of the community, they dug in. They began the rebuild before the embers of the fire went cold. The next year the new town celebrated when the CPR rolled into town.

MacLean would only serve two one-year terms. He was rewarded for his service with an appointment as stipendiary magistrate for Vancouver district in 1885. He would die the same. He was only 51 years old.

born person, first East Indian and first Muslim woman to be appointed to the Canadian Senate.

Also rising to prominence in Vancouver was Jamaica-born Rosemary

The XXI Olympiad

When the XXI Olympic Games open in Vancouver on February 12, 2010, the world's eyes will be on the city. For 17 days, 5,500 athletes and officials from more than 80 nations, 10,000 media representatives and 75 million visitors will descend on Vancouver. Around the world, 3 billion people will watch the games on TV.

The coming of the Olympiad has fuelled an unprecedented building boom as Olympic venues and facilities are being built across the city. Among these are the South East False Creek Athletes Village to house athletes, the Hillcrest Park Curling building (adjacent to Nat Bailey Stadium) and a new drug lab at Simon Fraser University.

Vancouver's transportation infrastructure is also on the grow. To accommodate the Games, Transit BC is adding a 19.5 km Canada Line, complete with 16 new stations, to the SkyTrain system. The Canada Line will see a tunnel built from Waterfront Station south to 64th Avenue, an elevated section going from 64th Avenue across the Fraser River to Richmond and west to the Vancouver Airport and central Richmond as well as a new Park and Ride facility at Bridgeport Station.

Given their magnitude and the profound impact they will have on the city, there has also been a good deal of debate surrounding the 2010 Games; they have become something of a political issue. Opponents voice concerns about a number of issues, including the high cost of the games. They suggest that the estimate put forth by Game organizers in March 2008 that suggests that the Games will cost $1.63 million is too low, noting that the figure does not include the estimated $600 million being spent on the Sea to Sky Highway between Vancouver and Whistler or the cost of upgrading Vancouver's transit system. Critics also worry about the Games' impact on the city's poor and the environment.

Supporters, meanwhile, contend that the Games' impact will be positive. They argue that costs will be offset by $436 million from TV revenue and $232 million in ticket sales and believe that that improvements to city infrastructure and economic opportunities will benefit all Vancouverites.

Brown, who was the first Black female elected to a legislature in Canada. Moving to her adopted home at age 21, Brown completed her university studies in Vancouver. In 1972 and in 1975 she was elected as the NDP MLA for Vancouver-Burrard. In 1979 and in 1983, she was elected for a different constituency. In 1975, Brown ran to lead the national NDPs. Although she lost on the fourth ballot, she was the first woman ever to run for the leadership of a federal party in Canada.

The career of Hong Kong-born, Vancouver-raised Jenny Kwan has also marked some firsts. In 1993, she was elected to the Vancouver City Council, at the time the youngest in history. She was one of the first Chinese-Canadians to sit in BC's provincial legislature, and was elected MLA for the Vancouver-Mount Pleasant riding in 1996, 2001 and again in 2005. In 1998, Kwan was appointed Minister of Municipal Affairs, becoming the province's first Chinese Canadian cabinet minister.

Sources: BC NDP; Parliament of Canada.

PROVINCIAL AND FEDERAL REPRESENTATION

- Provincial Legislature: 10 of 79 seats
- Canada House of Commons: 5 of 308 seats
- Senate of Canada: 2 of 105 seats (5 in total from BC)

Source: Parliament of Canada.

Weblinks

City Hall

vancouver.ca/cityhall/index.htm
Online home of Vancouver's City Hall, one of the city's most recognizable buildings. Here readers will learn of the building's history, heritage and legacy.

City of Vancouver Archives

vancouver.ca/ctyclerk/archives/index.htm
Learn more about Vancouver's political history.

Crime and Punishment

CRIMELINE

1869: Constable Tomkins Brew is assigned to police the booming Burrard Inlet area. When he asks for a police station and town jail, he gets a log cabin and two cells, strategically located near the Globe Saloon on the site of present day Gaoler's Mews.

1870: Twenty-two BCC officers are responsible for patrolling 250,000 square miles in British Columbia. The population at that time includes 5,782 white men, 2,794 white women, 297 black men, 165 black women, 1,495 Chinese men, 53 Chinese women and approximately 26,000 First Nations people.

1885: The Chinese Immigration Act subjects each Chinese immigrant to a head tax of $50. In 1900, the tax is increased to $100 and, in 1903, to $500.

1886: John Stewart is appointed the first — and for a time, the only — police constable in the new city of Vancouver.

1886: When a June 13 fire burns the city to the ground, Vancouver's police work out of a tent in Gastown. Criminals were chained to a tree stump.

1887: In July, a boot containing a foot and leg is found on the south side of False Creek, earning the neighbourhood its nickname: 'Leg-in-Boot Square.' The more things change…

1899: Seeking to stamp out prostitution, madams are fined $50 and 'working girls' $15, with half of each fine going to the police informant. Coincidentally, it is discovered that most tips came from a single employee of the Vancouver Police Department.

1904: Vancouver is home to 31 police officers and 27 jail cells, all of which are usually full.

1906: When an April 18 earthquake shakes San Francisco, many brothel madams move north to set up shop in Vancouver.

The Wild West

Settled largely by single young men who had risked it all to come west for gold or lives in the rough and tumble timber, mining or fishing industries, Gastown was literally afloat in booze. Liquor was in far greater supply than law and order, and the area became known for its drunken debauchery.

In 1858, the civil and criminal laws of Britain were applied to British Columbia. In an effort to instill order, Chartres Brew was appointed inspector of police and Matthew Baillie Begbie was proclaimed judge of the colony. The new officials attempted to bring in 150 trained police officers to BC, but succeeded in adding just 15 officers to the colony's policing. Not surprisingly, this miserly police presence had little impact. In 1871, desperate residents of Granville were still demanding a greater police presence to stem illicit activities at bars and newly opened bawdy houses. Only with Vancouver's incorporation did the town finally get a police officer.

Sporting Women

As a frontier gateway to the worlds of mining and logging, Vancouver was home to a disproportionate number of men. Living far from their families, they sought the comfort of women, and from the nineteenth century onwards there were enterprising women willing to provide companionship and comfort.

In the early 1870s, Birdie Stewart, an artist with an entrepreneurial spirit, opened Vancouver's first brothel on the corner of Water and Abbott Streets. Thus began a long heritage of "sporting women" in the city.

As this neighbourhood expanded, residents forced Stewart out and she set up her business in an Alexander Street rooming house. By 1904, Dupont Street (later renamed Pender) had emerged as Vancouver's "red light" district and in 1906 Chief of Police C.A. Chisholm reported that 41 brothels and 153 prostitutes were working in the region.

In an era of widespread social reform in the early 20th century, the city attempted to snuff out the red light district. In 1906, madams on Pender were ordered to shut down; in 1907, 136 women from the region were arrested, and 110 of them were convicted. A similar crackdown in Chinatown the following year saw police arrest another 71 working women. As police zeroed in, brothel owners branched out, opening businesses in new areas, and seeking more discrete business opportunities.

Over the years, prostitution in Vancouver, like the sex trade everywhere, has been resistant to law enforcement. By the 1950s, brothels had been replaced by a sex industry more quietly operated out of beer parlours and hotels.

This changed in 1975 when police raided the infamous Penthouse Night Club on Seymour Street. Critics charge that the mid-1970s crackdown on prostitution forced prostitutes back onto the streets. Today an estimated 2,000 sex-trade workers still operate in Vancouver.

Sources: History of Sex Work; Community Initiative for Health and Safety; Straight.com.

Take 5 CHRIS MATHIESON'S TOP FIVE
CRIMES IN VANCOUVER'S HISTORY

Chris Mathieson is the executive director of the Vancouver Police Museum. A fourth-generation Vancouverite, he has a strong interest in local history. His newest project, a city walking tour called "Sins of the City," has become a hit for those looking to catch a glimpse at Vancouver's history of vice.

1. **'Babes in the Woods' Murders:** The skeletons of two children between the ages of seven and ten were found in Stanley Park in 1953. They were both killed with a hatchet found nearby. This was an important point in Vancouver crime history as innovative forensic techniques were used in the case, including facial reconstruction. Still, the case went 'cold' and the evidence was stored away. Ten years later skeletal remains were subject to DNA testing and given a proper burial. As of 2007, the murders remain unsolved.

2. **The Murder of Janet Smith:** On July 26, 1924, the body of nurse-maid Janet Smith was found in her employer's home with a bullet in her brain and a gun in her hand. It was judged a self-inflicted, accidental death. Within a month, however, her body was exhumed and her death ruled a murder. Houseboy Wong Foon Sing, the only other person home at the time of the killing, became a suspect. On March 20, 1925, a group of men dressed in Klan-style robes kidnapped him and tortured him for six weeks. Reportedly, BC attorney general Alexander Manson knew of his whereabouts but did nothing. The kidnappers — who included police officers — failed to get a confession and released Wong. While Wong would later be arrested for murder, the case was thrown out for lack of evidence and Wong returned to China. Three of his kidnappers went to jail while the rest, including two police commissioners, were found not guilty. Despite accusations, rumours and theories — including corruption in high places, international intrigue and racism — the murder of Janet Smith has never been solved.

3. **The Castellani Murder:** Mrs. Esther Castellani had been ill for months so when she died of a supposed 'viral infection and heart attack' nothing seemed rotten in the city of Vancouver. A few months later a woman claimed she and the widower Rene Castellani had conspired to poison Esther with arsenic. Mrs. Castellani was exhumed and sure enough the dead woman's hair showed an uneven distribution of arsenic. The evidence suggested a gap in poisonings which happened to coincide with a week when the Mr. Castellani was away from home. Rene Castellani was sentenced to 25 years in prison in 1966 and was released after serving 13 years.

4. **The 'Missing Women':** Around 1983 women began to disappear from Vancouver's infamous Downtown Eastside, with an official tally of 65 missing. Most, if not all, of the missing women were associated with prostitution, drugs or both, which sadly meant that their disappearances went largely unnoticed. By the spring of 2005, Robert William "Willie" Pickton was charged with 26 counts of first-degree murder in relation to many of the missing women.

5. **The Pauls Family Murders:** On July 11, 1958, police visited the Pauls house after neighbours reported not seeing anyone from the family in two days. The police found 47-year-old Helen Pauls lying in the hallway in a pool of blood and at the end of the hallway the body of 12-year-old Dorothy Pauls. In the basement, David Pauls, 53, also lay in a pool of his own blood. Along with other forensic evidence was a partial footprint in the flower garden outside. Still, with no witnesses coming forward, no suspects and no motive, this unsolved triple murder is one of the city's most vexing.

> "So marked has been the decrease in minor crimes, especially drunkenness, since the advent of prohibition that the need for an auxiliary jail has ceased to exist."
>
> – *Vancouver Sun*, October 1917.

1907: In August, the Vancouver Police Department serves and protects with the help of its first automobile.

1907: An anti-Asian riot in the city, spurred by racist insistence that Asian immigrants are fostering an opium trade in order to weaken the "White Race," leads to the Opium Act, Canada's first national narcotic law.

1912: Nancy Harris and Minnie Miller become the first female police officers in Vancouver — and are even among the first in North America.

1912: On March 25, Constable Lewis Byers is the first Vancouver police officer killed in the line of duty when he responds to what should have been a routine "drunk annoying" call. His assailant, Oscar Larsen, is killed by police later that day.

1913: On May 28, Constable James Archibald is shot while trying to foil a burglary, becoming Vancouver's second officer killed in the line of duty.

1913: Joseph Smith, having been found guilty of murder in the death of a prison guard, is hanged at the BC Penitentiary. Smith's hanging is the only one to take place at that institution.

1917: Streets dry up as prohibition starts in British Columbia.

1919: Alex Ignace is the first of many to be hanged at Oakalla Prison Farm.

1920: In a July 15 raid, 14,000 gallons of whiskey are confiscated in what was the largest liquor seizure in Canadian history to that time. A week later the Vancouver Police Department advertise for burly men to move the impounded booze with a *Vancouver Sun* ad reading: "One dollar an hour and free smells at all broken bottles."

Malahat: A Rum Running Legend

Vancouver's position on the Pacific probably made its involvement in the illegal rum trade of the early 20th century inevitable. Washington State went dry in 1916, Canada banned alcohol in 1919 and in 1920 the Volstead Act instituted prohibition across the entire USA.

Although BC's prohibition was short-lived (it ended in 1920 and BC became the first province to institute state-controlled liquor sales), Americans would be thirsty until 1933. Enterprising Vancouverites with ships were happy between 1916 and 1933 to provide Americans with demon rum and, in the process, make a small fortune.

The most successful of Pacific rum-running ships was the Vancouver-based *Malahat*. Boasting a remarkable carrying capacity of 60,000 liquor cases, the Douglas fir-hulled vessel carried more contraband booze than any other vessel. On each rum-running excursion (each of which might last for a year), the *Malahat* anchored three miles off the US coast in international waters. Smaller American vessels would dock beside her, and the exchange of contraband would occur, safely outside the reach of American authorities.

The *Malahat's* career outlived prohibition. After 1933, the *Malahat* fulfilled another quintessentially West Coast duty — she became a log barge. When, in 1944, the *Malahat* took on water her sailing days were over. She was towed to Powell River where her sturdy frame became part of the breakwater.

They Said It

1921: Booze flows again in Vancouver as Prohibition ends. British Columbia sets a trend, becoming the first province to offer government-controlled liquor sales.

1924: The body of Scottish nursemaid Janet Smith is discovered in her employer's home. Initially deemed an accidental suicide, her friends convince authorities that the 22-year-old would not have killed herself, and her death is ruled a murder. When the murder goes unsolved for months, an outraged public picks a predictable scapegoat — a Chinese houseboy, Wong Foon Sing. Sing is kidnapped and tortured by vigilantes, but the innocent man refuses to confess. Smith's murder has never been solved.

1929: The police departments of Point Grey, South Vancouver and Vancouver amalgamate.

1937: The *Vancouver Province* reports that marijuana traces had been found in a dead man's stomach, marking the first time the word 'marijuana' is used in a local paper.

1939: The *Vancouver News Herald* estimates there are 50 'blind pigs' in Vancouver, paltry compared to the more than 3,000 illegal drinking establishments in Montreal.

1939: Canada's first Elizabeth Fry Society is established in Vancouver.

Vancouver's Opium Wars

The 19th century gave rise to a global drug trade in opium (a drug derived from the poppy plant) and the Chinese used the drug for pain and pleasure. Even when Chinese rulers banned opium, England supplied opium to China in return for tea leaves (later, the two nations would wage wars over the drug).

By the time the first Chinese came to Vancouver in the mid 19th century, opium was part of the community. Low-paying (and seasonal) jobs in the woods, mines and on the railroad forced Chinese immigrants to live in poverty. Opium was an acceptable way to ease boredom and in Canada it was entirely legal until 1907.

For a time BC relished the opium trade. When San Francisco imposed a tax on opium in the 1870s, opium bound for the American West Coast was routed through Vancouver and other BC communities and for a while became the province's third largest export to the United States (after coal and fur).

Opium dens abounded in Chinatown and were frequented by Chinese and non-Chinese alike. The use of opium by Anglo-saxon Canadians flamed existing anti-Chinese sentiment and by the early 20th century a chorus of urban reformers were decrying the drug.

One of the loudest voices was that of Emily Murphy, the same woman who helped win the Person's Case and became Canada's first female police magistrate. In a series of popular articles published in *Maclean's* magazine Murphy charged that the opium trade was part of a deliberate Chinese tactic to undermine the stability of society and the purity of the "white race." It was not her finest moment.

Murphy's charges found resonance in Vancouver — and across Canada for that matter. A series of federal laws were passed in an attempt to quell opium use. The 1908 Opium Narcotic Act (and its successors) prohibited the import, manufacture and sale of opiates — but also but had an additional not-so-subtle aim of limiting Chinese immigration.

In spite of anti-opium legislation, police had a difficult time stemming its use. In 1922, the RCMP estimated that Vancouver was home to 2,200 opium addicts who consumed 119,360 ounces of opium a year. Although Vancouver had a RCMP drug squad, it consisted of just three non-commissioned officers and six constables and relied heavily on "snitches." Opium would prove impossible to route and by the time it diminished new drugs has found their way on to the street.

"In the confirmed white smoker of opium, changes in the face always take place. The skin becomes more adherent to the facial muscles, whose fat has been partly absorbed. It assumes a yellow, ivory-like colour, more pronounced about the cheek bones. These, because of the shrinkage of facial fat, appear accentuated. There is slowly developed Mongolian or Chinese expression that discloses to the informed the cause of such metamorphosis. The "opium look" often gives an insight to an otherwise unsuspected habit."

– A 1935 RCMP quarterly report that shows the connection between racism and the anti-opium campaign in Canada. According to the RCMP, white opium users are readily recognizable because, of course, they start to look Asian!

1953: The remains of two murdered children and the murder weapon (a hatchet) are found in Stanley Park hidden beneath a fur coat. The "Babes in the Woods" murders have never been solved.

1955: Chief Constable Walter Mulligan is investigated for political corruption. Adding to suspicions of his guilt, midway through the investigation Mulligan flees for California.

1959: Leo Mantha is the last person hanged at BC's Oakalla Prison before capital punishment is abolished.

Did you know...

that evidence in the Pickton murder trial consisted of more than 40,000 crime scene photos, 235,000 seized items, 600,000 lab exhibits, half a million pages of documents and the testimony of 98 witnesses?

Beast of British Columbia

Vancouver has the dubious distinction of being home to one Canada's most notorious serial killers. In the early 1980s Clifford Olson terrorized the city.

The teenaged Olson had frequent run-ins with the law and by age 21 had been arrested 94 times. On Christmas Day, 1980, the body of a 12-year-old Surrey girl was found. She would be just the first of Olson's young victims. In all, the murder and assault of eight girls and three boys aged nine to 18 have been pegged on Olson.

Well-known to police, Olson became a suspect in the serial killings early in the investigation and police remain troubled that four of his victims were murdered while Olson was under police surveillance. Only in August 1981 did his murderous spree end in arrest.

The controversy did not end there. On his detainment, Olson struck a controversial deal with provincial officials that angered many Canadians, especially victims' families. In a deal crassly dubbed "cash for corpses," Olson negotiated for a $100,000 trust fund to be paid to his wife and child in return for his cooperation in locating his victims' remains.

Clifford Olson was convicted of 11 counts of first-degree murder and sentenced to life in prison. The judge recommended he never be granted parole. Decades after his crimes, Olson reportedly shows no remorse. He has boasted of having committed an additional 80 to 200 murders and promised that, if released, "the beast of British Columbia," as he styles himself, will kill again.

In July of 2006, Olson was again denied parole; it is expected that this will be the case again in 2008. Still, Olson manages to infuriate his victims' families and all Canadians. In May 2008, Canadians were shocked to learn that Olson maintained a MySpace web page that listed as his "friends" such serial killers as Charles Manson and Charles Ng.

1971: People dedicated to the legalization of marijuana hold a 'smoke-in' in Gastown. When police move in to break it up, a riot erupts. When the dust settles, 79 people are arrested and 38 charged.

1980: On Christmas Day the body of a 12-year-old girl, the first known victim of serial killer Clifford Olson, is found.

1982: Clifford Olson pleads guilty to 11 counts of murder and is handed 11 concurrent life sentences.

1985: On June 20, a man walks into a Canadian Pacific airline office and buys two tickets, one under the name M. Singh from Vancouver to Montreal and one under the name L. Singh from Vancouver to Tokyo. Two days later Air India Flight 182 explodes in the air over the coast of Ireland, killing all 329 people on board.

1989: A Russian gang is routed by the Vancouver Police Department. Police seize more than 13 kg of cocaine, machine guns and high-end autos.

2002: Robert William "Willie" Pickton is charged with two counts of first-degree murder connected to a string of women who had gone missing from Vancouver's downtown Eastside over the previous two decades. Three years later Pickton is charged with 27 counts of first degree murder. In the summer of 2006, the presiding judge decides that Pickton will stand trial for six counts, the remainder to be possibly tried later.

2007: Willie Pickton is found guilty of six counts of second-degree murder and is sentenced to life without parole for 25 years, the same sentence he would have received had he been found guilty of murder in the first-degree.

2008: Inderjit Singh Reyat, the only person convicted in the Air India bombing case, is released on $500,000 bail.

They Said It

"For the most part, kids involved here are people who come from middle-class and upper-class homes. They get involved for the glamour."

– Wallace T. Oppal, Court of Appeal of British Columbia, commenting on gang involvement in Vancouver.

RECENT NUMBERS

Preliminary statistics for 2007 indicate that crime was down in Vancouver over 2006. Violent crime dropped by six percent, property crime by 10.9 percent, and all other crimes were down by 6.8 percent. Police also had fielded 27,658 fewer calls in 2007 over 2006.

Source: City of Vancouver.

The Farm

In early February 2002, police cordoned off most of a Port Coquitlam pig farm and began excavating. Police were tight-lipped, but rumours circulated that the excavation was connected to the dozens of missing women from Vancouver's notorious Downtown Eastside.

The rumours were true. Within a year, Pickton was indicted on 26 counts of first-degree murder. The court proceedings began in January 2006. Justice James Williams took nearly a year to rule on what evidence could and could not be presented to a jury. In August, Justice Williams decided it would be just too much for one jury to hear and so he decided to split the charges and have Pickton answer only to six counts during this first trial.

The Pickton trial resumed in January 2007 and on December 9, the jury returned verdicts of not guilty on all six charges of first-degree murder, and guilty on all six charges of second-degree murder. Two days later, Justice Williams sentenced Pickton to life in prison without the possibility of parole for 25 years. Robert Pickton is charged with 20 additional counts of murder, with a decision pending on whether or not he will stand trial for them.

CRIME IN VANCOUVER

Vancouver's crime rate is in the middle of the pack of rates compared to other Canadian urban centres, with the exception of break-ins, which are more common here. In 2006, the Vancouver Police Department (VPD) received 271,549 calls for service, up 3.7 percent over 2005. For every 100,000 citizens there were:

- 2.9 homicides (4.3 in Edmonton; 1.3 in Montreal)
- 149 robberies (263 in Winnipeg; 88 in Ottawa)
- 1,192 break-ins (1,025 in Edmonton; 388 in Toronto)
- 990 motor vehicle thefts (1,712 in Winnipeg; 306 in Toronto)

Sources: Statistics Canada; City of Vancouver.

VIOLENT CRIME (7,963, UP 6.1 PERCENT FROM 2005)

- 15 culpable homicides (down 21.1 percent)
- 13 attempted murder (down 23.5 percent)
- 528 sexual offences (down 1.3 percent)
- 5,775 assaults (up 6.7 percent)
- 1,632 robberies (up 7.2 percent)
- 8 abductions

Did you know...

that the Lower Eastside has the dubious distinction of being home to the highest HIV infection rates in North America?

They Said It

"Most of the violence being encountered in our communities is directly associated to the production, distribution and consumption of illegal drugs. Targeting organized crime groups is one of our top priorities."

– Al Macintyre, Assistant Commissioner
Officer in Charge, Criminal Operations Branch, BC RCMP.

PROPERTY CRIME (49,736, DOWN 4.7 PERCENT FROM 2005)

- 8,655 break and enters (up 3.4 percent)
- 26,784 thefts under $5,000 (down 19 percent)
- 526 thefts over $5,000 (down 6 percent)
- 1,507 possessions of stolen goods (down 19.1 percent)
- 2,160 cases of fraud (up 15.8 percent)
- 302 cases of arson (up 34.2 percent)
- 5,463 cases of mischief over/under $5,000 (up 7.8 percent)

The Forgotten Women

The known victims of Willie Pickton are among the dozens who are called The Forgotten Women—women, many of whom are Aboriginal, whose lives on society's margin have made their disappearances "invisible" to society at large.

Some people are out to change this and artist Pamela Masik is one of them. Masik plans to paint portraits of all 69 women who police say have disappeared from the Downtown Eastside since 1978. The website http://missingpeople.net is another initiative seeking to return identities to the forgotten women. Row upon row of photographs show their faces, and by clicking on each image one can read their biographies and, as the website explains, "understand a bit about who they were as people."

Take 5 — TOP FIVE STOLEN
MAKES AND MODELS

1. **Dodge Caravan/Plymouth Voyager**
2. **Honda Civic**
3. **Ford F-Series**
4. **Honda Accord**
5. **Dodge/Plymouth Neon**

Source: Insurance Corporation of BC.

OTHER CRIME (12,230 UP 20.9 PERCENT FROM 2005)

- 285 cases of prostitution (down 21.5 percent)
- 1 gaming and betting charge (down 75 percent)
- 1,611 offensive weapons charges (up 15.6 percent)

Source: City of Vancouver.

POLICING VANCOUVER

In 2005, there were 148 police officers for every 100,000 citizens in Vancouver CMA. This compares to the national rate of 192, and to these rates in other urban centres: 185 in Winnipeg, 184 in Montreal, 173 in Toronto and 157 in Halifax.

- Gross expenditures for 2006: $159.3 million
- In 2006 there were 1,582 people working for the VPD — 1,214 police offers and 368 civilians.

STOLEN CARS

In 2006, there were 4,338 car thefts in the city of Vancouver — which means there were 751 cars stolen for every 100,000 citizens. That's down from the city's 2005 rate of 990, which, at the time, compared

Did you know...

that 37 percent of all cars stolen in British Columbia in 2006 were taken from the streets of Vancouver?

TOP FIVE NEIGHBOURHOODS
FROM WHICH CARS WERE STOLEN IN VANCOUVER
IN 2007 (Percentage of total stolen)

1. **Central Business District** (16 percent)
2. **Grandview Woodlands** (8 percent)
3. **Fairview** (7 percent)
4. **Kitsilano** (7 percent)
5. **Mount Pleasant** (7 percent)

Source: Vancouver Police Department.

with other large city rates of 1,712 for Winnipeg and 260 for Quebec City, and with smaller city rates of 1,514 in neighbouring Abbotsford and 137 for Saint John, New Brunswick.

Source: Statistics Canada.

MOTOR VEHICLE
In Vancouver in 2006, there were:
- 1,394 traffic accidents, 20 of which were fatal
- 1,243 traffic accidents that caused property damage
- 15,000 auto break-ins
- 39 charges of dangerous operation of a motor vehicle
- 2,065 charges of impaired driving
- 112 charges of failing or refusing to give a breath or blood sample
- 106 charges of failing to stop or remain at the scene of an accident
- 94 charges of driving while prohibited

Sources: Vancouver Police Department; Insurance Corporation of British Columbia.

CORRECTIONAL FACILITIES
- Number of correctional centres in BC: 9
- Number in Greater Vancouver: 2
- The Metro Vancouver correction facilities, the North Fraser Pretrial

Centre and the Surrey Pretrial Services Centre are high security facilities designed to house those awaiting trial.

Source: Government of British Columbia.

SAFE INJECTION, SAFE FOR NOW

In 2007, InSite, North America's first supervised safe injection site, was established to provide Vancouver drug addicts a clean place to inject themselves and a gateway into detox. Exempted from Canada's Controlled Drugs and Substances Act, the federal government opposed the program and challenged it in a BC Supreme Court case. In May 2008 this court ruled that the closure of the safe injection site would be unconstitutional and granted the program a continued exemption from federal drug laws.

Weblinks

Vancouver Police Museum

www.vancouverpolicemuseum.ca

The Vancouver Police Museum takes visitors back in time into the city's crime and criminal history, as well as the history of those who tried to clean it all up.

Vancouver Police Department

www.city.vancouver.bc.ca/police/

The online home of the Vancouver Police Department is a great source to find out more about the state of crime in the city today.

British Columbia Crime Prevention Association

www.bccpa.org/

This group is made up of both citizens and police who are dedicated to preventing crime all over the province. A plethora of information and resources, education and awareness are the main goals here.